T0193620

WHERE ARE THE *Heroes?*

PENNY RUTH

WESTBOW
PRESS®
A DIVISION OF THOMAS NELSON
& ZONDERVAN

Scripture taken from the Holy Bible, NEW INTERNATIONAL VERSION®.
Copyright © 1973, 1978, 1984, 2011 by Biblica, Inc. All rights reserved worldwide.
Used by permission. NEW INTERNATIONAL VERSION® and NIV® are
registered trademarks of Biblica, Inc. Use of either trademark for the offering
of goods or services requires the prior written consent of Biblica US, Inc.

WestBow Press books may be ordered through booksellers or by contacting:

WestBow Press
A Division of Thomas Nelson & Zondervan
1663 Liberty Drive
Bloomington, IN 47403
www.westbowpress.com
1 (866) 928-1240

Because of the dynamic nature of the Internet, any web addresses or links contained in
this book may have changed since publication and may no longer be valid. The views
expressed in this work are solely those of the author and do not necessarily reflect the
views of the publisher, and the publisher hereby disclaims any responsibility for them.

Any people depicted in stock imagery provided by Thinkstock are models,
and such images are being used for illustrative purposes only.
Certain stock imagery © Thinkstock.

ISBN: 978-1-9736-1748-8 (sc)
ISBN: 978-1-9736-1749-5 (hc)
ISBN: 978-1-9736-1747-1 (e)

Library of Congress Control Number: 2018901187

Print information available on the last page.

WestBow Press rev. date: 01/30/2018

Contents

Thank you Molly, my dear daughter, for your patience, encouragement, and knowledge.

INTRODUCTION

Christians come in all shapes and sizes, and we all walk in different levels of faith. I am fifty-seven years old and have been a Christian for twenty years. I am no expert on faith, religion, or the Bible. The following pages simply present some of my observations, opinions, experiences, and desires in relation to the worldwide church. I have included some poetic messages that I believe are from God.

I had always thought that those who attended church on Sunday were perfect, or at least good. I don't know why I thought that; I just did. I had it in my mind that those people had grown up saintly and were the clean people loved by God.

There are children who grow up in terrible situations, even amid life-threatening conditions. No matter how dire your personal situation may be or may have been, there is someone in this world suffering through worse. There are real heroes who may not leap tall buildings in a single bound, but they do deny themselves for the sake of others. These heroes lose sleep and miss a meal or two for your sake. Real heroes don't need a mask or a costume; they walk in the power and anointing of the Holy Spirit. They reflect Jesus.

Where Are the Heroes? contains portions of my own testimony, which is to be distinguished from my story. A story can be anything you want it to be, but a testimony is a truthful account of God's transforming power and unconditional love. Stories about us tend to be filled with blame, accusations, excuses, and self-pity, along with a bit of exaggeration and lots of drama. A testimony consists of a victorious account of all the ways God has changed your heart, your head, your mouth, and your direction. God's vision becomes your vision, and His love begins to overwhelm your heart. Whatever your story is, no matter what you have been through, Jesus is the key to victory—and the victory comes through repentance.

Where Are the Heroes?

The church is called to change the world.
Where are the heroes?
How many people got saved last week?
Care to take a peek?

The census is down;
The coffee's not ground;
The floors are starting to creak.

Who's in control of your hodgepodge mirage?
What do you truly seek?

Do you encourage the meek and walk with the weak,
Or do you offer a future that's bleak?

Faith can make a mountain move and put a cancer to sleep.
Faith can build a friendly bridge that leads into the deep.
Faith is not for onetime use; it's something that we keep.

It's hard for you to see the wolves
When you're busy counting sheep.

†

A hero is someone who faces danger or rejection for the sake of others, who stands up for the weak and the meek, who tells the truth even if it hurts, who walks in righteousness when it is not popular to do so, who makes time, who is patient, and who allows you to be who you are in Christ.

Looking over the last twenty years, I do not find it hard to point out my heroes. I was born again in 1997, and it was no coincidence that Jane Becker was the first person I saw right afterward. I had become acquainted with Terry and Jane Becker, who had bought the house across the street from me four or five years earlier. They moved in after my family and I had lived there for about a year. The Beckers had a group of people they met with every Wednesday night for Bible study and prayer. Little did I know that I was the one they were praying for.

For about five years Jane would come visit me and would patiently listen to me talk, talk, talk. Jane smiled a lot and had such a peace about her. I thought she was weird. My life was anything but peaceful, and I cussed and fussed much more than I smiled. I was always happy to see her walk over, but I was also relieved when she left. Jane did not quote scripture to me or even invite me to church; she was just nice—and she had that tormenting peace.

I thank God that Jane and Terry did not give up on me or on the power of the Holy Spirit. They knew how tough it would be for me to surrender, but they understood God's power through prayer. That small group of people who faithfully prayed for my family had no idea how God would respond. They simply had faith that He would.

I have four brothers whom at that point I had not seen in years, and I had no idea if any of them were Christians. My oldest brother, Brad, called to tell me that he had been born again and saying that he needed to see me. I did not trust him. He wouldn't give up, so after several phone calls I relented. When I saw my brother, he pulled me in for a long hug. I knew right then that there had been a change and that it was genuine. We spent the day together, and he read to me from the Bible while sharing testimonies of how the Holy Spirit was transforming his life. It was very weird but wonderful to hear him talk this way. My brother had hope and joy for the first time in his life. Oh, and there was that peace, the same peace I'd seen in Terry and Jane. Brad told me that God had reminded him that he had a sister and said that he was to get in touch with me.

It was on my drive home from Brad's house that I cried out for Jesus to save me. And when I pulled up to my house, Jane was sitting out on her drive. I walked over and told her that I got it. She said, "Got what?" I repeated, "I got it." She started crying because she could see it. She recognized the peace, the same peace that I had seen in my brother and that I saw in her.

Jane became my sister, my best friend, and my first prayer partner, and for a time she, Terry, and Brad were my only support. They had to put up with my many calls a day loaded with questions and excitement, but they were very encouraging. Brad, Terry, and Jane were all fairly new Christians, so we were learning together and pushing each other into the Word, worship, and prayer. My brother Brad is one of my best friends today. The credit for that credit goes to God, the Restorer.

Terry Becker died in January 2016, in the Philippines, one week after giving his youngest daughter's hand in marriage. He was a wonderful friend and encourager, and a special husband and father, and he loved the Lord with his whole heart. He always wanted to know what God was showing me. Terry encouraged everyone to dream bigger. I miss you, friend.

†

TERRY

The man who swims between the shore,
Who dives into the deep,

His life will reap forevermore;
His family God will keep.

The treasure stored in heaven
Will fill his earthly chest.

He tends his garden on the earth
And builds an eagle's nest,

A place for him to rest.

This man has learned to trust
In One he cannot see.

He lives inside the worship
That feeds his family tree.

A godly man is all he cares to be.

†

Terry was a man after God's heart. Whether he was in his office or in the yard, he had worship music playing. He steeped himself in worship and in the Word. Terry didn't just provide for and feed his family; he also planted seed, in obedience, wherever he walked.

Ezekiel 47:1 provides a picture of a life lived in spirit and in truth, in obedience and surrender. This is a picture of the blessed and fruitful life of one who takes the plunge, casts off all doubt, and reaps the rewards of faithfulness.

I think of the many times people have come to me frustrated and exhausted from ministering to someone who showed no signs of change. I think of how frustrating I must have been to Terry and Jane, yet they never gave up on me. They and their small group prayed for me for five years. I am very grateful for their steadfast faith and hope.

LORD

Would you defend the likes of me?

Would you take my case and waive the fee?

Would you hide me beneath your tree?

Will you rescue me?

Would you choose me for eternity?

Would you fight for me against an enemy that I can't see?

Will you pull me in when the ship goes down?

Will you wash my face when I look like a clown?

Will you feed me, clothe me, sing me to sleep?

Will you correct me when I'm in too deep?

Will you count me as one of your sheep?

The Way I Talk

I'm mean;
I'm loud;
I talk real hard.
I'm surprised they gave me a library card.

I pray for a mouth that's tame and sweet,
Paired with a voice that's real petite.

I'm afraid I'm a lot like Pete.

There's a place on earth for all to serve,
But God doesn't grade on a curve.

Some folks follow others their entire life.
Some folks live for their husband or wife.

Some folks take pride in their cars and their jobs.
Some folks live like lazy slobs.

I have one interest, one hobby to date.
He likes how I talk and how I relate.

He's the reason I'm loud
(It's not that I'm proud).
He's the reason I'm free
And able to see.

He's the reason I'm able
To finally be me.

†

I wrote this poem with my friend Lynn Nieman in mind. She lived for the Lord and she displayed His loving-kindness, gentle spirit, and grace. Lynn prayed like the valiant warrior God had created her to be. She was well loved by some but mocked by others; she was admired but also despised. Lynn lived with an attitude of praise and thanksgiving, and she used her mouth to bless, not to curse. She will always be a hero to me. The two of us will praise God together in heaven one day.

The Wedding Day

The garment is chosen,
A perfect fit.

The oil is full;
The lamps are lit.

The church is dressed in her best attire.
The Bridegroom awaits;
His heart is on fire.

Vows were written long ago,
Displayed for all to see.

This courtship led to romance,
Despite the powers that be.

On this day the two become one.
All plans are put to rest.

He speaks the words she longs to hear:

Beloved,
Well done.
Come live beneath my vest.

Lynn was introduced to me in 1998, about a year after I was born again. She was my prayer partner for ten years, but we were very different from one another. Lynn was somewhat older than I and had been a Christian for many years. She was full of joy but was also constantly tormented. Lynn was in love with the Lord and very much in tune with the Holy Spirit, but she was discouraged by the church and the world around her. Lynn knew the Word, and she could teach it. She was always smiling, whereas I was serious. She loved working with children, whereas I loved working with adults. She could sing; I cannot. One thing we had in common was prayer. We were like a well-oiled machine when we interceded together. She helped me to understand travail, baptism in the Holy Spirit, praying in tongues, and prophecy. She was confirmation when I needed it and correction when I needed to be rebuked. I loved her very much. Lynn was a mother figure for me, the fun aunt, an older sister, a best friend. God knows how to fill the gaps in our lives, and fortunately for me I was assigned to Lynn. Thank you, Jesus! Lynn went to be with the Lord on May 15, 2009, at the age of sixty-two. I miss her dearly.

Bob and Jill Jones offered strong biblical teaching. They not only encouraged spiritual depth and propriety but also started a prayer team at my new church. A prayer team was something I had been praying for, and Bob and Jill were the perfect pair to lead it. It was an honor to sit under their leadership, not only in the prayer and altar ministry team but also in Sunday school. I learned so much from them both. I could call Jill anytime with any question, and she would come over or we would meet somewhere. I knew that Jill would be honest with me. She was more concerned about my faith than about my feelings. That is love.

We are to learn from, to listen to, and to obey the Holy Spirit, but there will be times when the Spirit of God speaks to us through Sunday school teachers like Dave and Deb Price, through new friends like Jill Carpenter, Joy Kirby, Tim and Renee Cotter, and Cheryl Carson, and through prophets traveling through town like Bill Otten and René from Honduras. I encourage you to remember key people in your life. Remember God's timing and all the ways He has used each person to help you to become who you are today.

I am giving credit to people, although I know that without the Holy Spirit they would not have been significant in my life. They took the time to learn the Word and to form a real relationship with God. These are people who have been transformed and been proven obedient. I am sure that they too have at least one hero in their lives who gave them encouragement and direction.

Watchman Nee (deceased), Joyce Meyer, Mike Bickle, and Jim Cymbala have written books that have changed my life. Worship through IHOP, Kansas City, Missouri, and Bethel, Redding, California; David Crowder; Kari Jobe; Hillsong; have drawn me into warfare, repentance, desire, compassion, adoration, and even deliverance. It is so important to listen to music that is honoring to God and encourages a deeper relationship with Him. Worship not only feeds your spirit; it also blesses the Lord and creates intimacy between you and Him.

IS YOUR FATHER YOUR HERO?

If you were in trouble, could you go to your father and count on him to make things right for you? If you needed to be encouraged, or if you needed money, or if you just needed a hug, would you go to your father?

My father was never allowed to look at me, talk to me, or have any kind of relationship with me. I never sat on his lap. He never hugged me, never told me he loved me, nothing. Mother would threaten him with bodily harm if he paid any attention to me at all. If she wanted me to be spanked with the belt, she made Dad do it, but that was all the interaction I had with him until I was an adult and she kicked him out. Dad broke down and confessed things that she had done to me as an infant. He asked for my forgiveness for not helping me. He said he had five children and he feared my mother would leave him.

I am not looking for sympathy, because I am not pathetic. I am God's dear daughter. I share bits of my past to let you know that God is making use of my life regardless of the past. I started running toward Him the day I got saved, and I have never looked back. I talk with Him because He is with me wherever I go. I include God in my life, and I try to let Him lead it. I worship Him with my words, money, ministry, and obedience. I make a lot of mistakes, but He picks me up and brushes me off and we start again. Jesus is my hero. I needed to be loved, but I did not know what love looked like until I met my Savior.

If you grew up with parents who loved you, fed you, and encouraged you, tell them thank you. Hug them and tell them how much you appreciate the safe, secure environment they provided for you. Be kind to your parents, pray for them, and be there whenever they need you.

MY FATHER, MY HERO

Are you the light of your Father's eye?
Did he kiss your boo-boos when you would cry?

Did he answer your every how, when, and why?

Did your father call you princess
Or the smartest girl in the world?

Did he say that you were pretty?
Did he watch you when you twirled?

Did your father build your Barbie house
Or protect you from a giant mouse?

Was he praying for your future,
Or for your future spouse?

Fathers bless their daughters
In many different ways.
Just by lending an ear, shedding a tear,
And cherishing all the days.

No matter if there's money
Or if your father's poor,
Blessings from a righteous man
Will open wisdom's door.

Real Danger or Fictional Fantasy?

To most children, superheroes are fictional comic book characters. Hananiah, Azariah, and Mishael were real men who walked into a blazing furnace and emerged without a burn. Noah listened to God and saved his family. Jonah finally obeyed and saved Nineveh. Esther obeyed God and saved the entire nation of Israel. David killed a giant with a slingshot. Daniel was thrown into a den of hungry lions yet came out alive.

When we portray witches, warlocks, and vampires as heroes, we are exalting the demonic. Witchcraft is real and dangerous. There is no such a thing as "good" witchcraft, so in book or movie scenes you sometimes have a demonic figure slaying a dragon, which is an oxymoron. Billions of dollars are spent each year on necromancy, sorcery, divination, mysticism, and fantasy. Our children and our young adults are being led down a very dangerous road. Teachers decorate the classrooms with witches, ghosts, and goblins, yet they are prohibited from saying or displaying "Merry Christmas" or referencing Christ in any way to celebrate Christmas.

Today's church is filled with people finding love through online dating, eliminating an untimely or inconvenient pregnancy, engaging in extramarital affairs, and working to pay credit card bills.

Christians don't have to wait on God anymore, because money pretty much buys everything. We don't have to develop patience. We want it our way, and we want it now. We live in a world where the idea of growing old gracefully is frightening, and where the almighty dollar overrules the Almighty.

THE LEAST DESIRABLE CANDIDATE

I had to be the least desirable candidate for salvation, but I am saved because God's mercy is more powerful than my sin. I cussed like a sailor and drank like one too. I have done many regrettable things in my life, but I knew the minute He touched me that I was forgiven. It took a year, spending time alone with the Lord, fasting and praying, and studying the Word, before I was finally able to forgive myself.

I vowed not to be like my mother, but there were underlying traits waiting to be unleashed. I was paranoid and jealous and always chasing the dollar. I practiced necromancy and sorcery on a regular basis and used my mouth to curse, lie, and gossip. Does that sound like a saint to you?

I grew up poor and at one time lived in a house with no indoor plumbing. Our bathroom was an outhouse crawling with daddy-long-legs! My mother was in and out of the hospital "resting," and I carried a lot of false responsibility. I suffered with ulcers from about the age of ten. The second-born child, I had four brothers. I did all the housework and laundry and cared for the two youngest boys as much as I could.

For as long as I can remember, I was "the girl" (insert expletives between *the* and *girl*). My mother referred to me that way often and told me that she'd never wanted a daughter. She said that God was punishing her and that's why she had me. She was constantly hitting me, pulling my hair, slapping my face or mouth, or twisting my nose while telling me that she couldn't stand to look at me. She humiliated me many times and told me that I would never amount to anything, that I was stupid and a liar. I spent thirty-seven years seeking Mother's love and approval, but I never received it. I grew up thinking there must be something terribly wrong with me. If Mother could find nothing good in me, then surely everyone I met would eventually come to the same conclusion. If Mother couldn't love me, how could the Creator of the Universe?

The first words spoken to me by God were "Dear Daughter."

Daughter

A daughter is a blessing, not a curse,
A gift from God, a prophetic verse,

Someone to laugh with and be your friend,
The pride of your life from beginning to end.

A daughter is a daughter no matter the way,
Through marriage or birth, or on adoption day.

What more can I say?

Hold her close for as long as you can.
Pray and fast for a righteous man to take her hand.

Tell her she's smart and pretty too.
Tell her she's blessed and loved by you.

Tell her she can do that which she puts her mind to.

Teach your daughter that there is a road,
A right and a wrong, a truth to be told.

Tell her about the days of old.
Pray and fast for a future that's bright.
Pray that she'll answer her call and shine the light,

That all will be well and her heart will be right.

Children are gifts, so handle with care.
We fight for their futures. We stand and declare,

"This one's for Jesus!

Devil, beware."

Every Child

Every girl needs to know that she is someone's daughter. Everyone needs to know that they were wanted by their parents. Every child needs to know that their mother loves them, and every child needs their father's blessing.

Children are tossed away like trash. Some are neglected and abused by their parents or other family members, and some children are spoiled to the point of being rotten and intolerable. Everyone has a different story, and everyone has a different testimony.

I admire single women who raise respectful children. It cannot be an easy thing to do. Every child needs their father's blessing; however, some fathers bless their children by staying away! Many people reproduce and give birth, but not everyone is a parent.

I grew up around much abuse and prejudice, but I have been redeemed by the blood of Jesus. I have been given a fresh start and a chance to produce blessings for future generations. I am the beginning of a new bloodline. I will never use my past as an excuse, but I will use it as a weapon of overcoming and victory for God.

My children know that they are loved, as will my grandchildren. There will be no discrimination or division in my family tree if I can help it. I was terrified that I would be cruel and abusive because my mother was, but I never had that in me. When my husband felt that a spanking was necessary for one of our children, I would have to go to another room and shut the door, unable to stand to listen to it. Sometimes I would even cry. I would then go in and explain to my children why they had gotten the spanking. My husband certainly didn't abuse my children, but he did teach them respect and obedience. My children rarely had to be disciplined because their father was willing to do it when it was needed.

My husband blesses our children, and they respect and love their father. This has made it much easier for my girls to accept God as Father.

They have a healthy relationship with their natural father, which gives them a positive and respectful opinion of men and makes it possible for them to love and trust Abba Father.

Our children grow up knowing what we tell them, and they trust us because we are the parent. So if we tell our children there is a Santa Claus, they believe it. If we tell our children they are stupid, they believe that as well. Our words have the power to plant seeds of insecurity, worry, doubt, fear, paranoia, low self-esteem, anger, and so much more. Our words also have the power to plant seeds of security, joy, peace, respect, love, grace, mercy, responsibility, integrity, and justice. I could go on.

Children are not ignorant, and they are watching us. Children have more discernment than many of the adults I know. Just ask a child to pray for you and you will be moved. God will not only take notice and lean in but He will answer.

Children are attracted to heroism and associate themselves with particular superheroes. Children need to know that there is goodness, integrity, protection, truth, justice, and honor within real people. How is it that Hollywood understands the demonic and that comic book creators understand righteousness better than most Christians do?

Love Is ...

A hopeful view,
A praiseful tongue,

The best review.

Love is a hug, a touch, or a word.
Love is an ear when you need to be heard.

Love is the action when there's no time to pray.
Love is reacting in a peculiar way.

When you are abandoned by all, love will stay,
Even on a rainy day.

Love is hope spread out like a cover.
It is to stand in faith for a sister or a brother.

Love is a fast and is always the truth.
It stands in the gap and prays for our youth.

Love is a person who took up my cross.
He didn't consider or count it a loss;

He just carried my cross.

Where Do I Fit?

For much of my life I allowed my circumstances to define who I was, who I would become, and how I felt that others viewed me. God changed all that. In one day I was set free and saw the world much differently. Yes, it has taken years to heal the wounds and to change my mind, but we never stop growing in the Lord. We become better servants and brighter lights for Him if we allow the truth to surface, if we allow shame to dissipate, if we allow regrets to fall behind, and if we surrender ourselves to Him daily. Who I had become was ugly and hard, and I had lost hope.

Today I only want to serve the Lord, but unfortunately I am discouraged to do so by organized churches. I have a faith that is way bigger than I am, and I am aggrieved much of the time. People tell me to stop whining and to get somewhere and serve, adding that no church is perfect. I am well aware of all that, given that I am not perfect either, but I need a church that fits with me and that is a place where God can use me and where human beings won't try to control the prophetic.

When I say organized churches, I don't mean that you can't organize your services and have policies in place. What I mean is that you are so organized that you forget to give the Holy Spirit His place. We forget that it is God's building and God's sheep. Although we have been entrusted with these things, we should never forget our place.

Does God (the Holy Spirit) have room to function in your services or through you?

In your church, how many people got saved in the last three months, or how many got baptized who were really saved? Do you know which of your leaders are spiritual and which are not? Are you spiritual? Do you know what being spiritual means?

I am not a religion. I cut my hair short and wear makeup and pants, but I also speak in tongues. I don't speak in tongues loudly so as to make a nuisance of myself or cause confusion, but I do use my prayer language frequently. God would never bring confusion into a meeting, but people do, because people desire attention and adoration. It is not about us. Let me say it again: It is not about us. It is not by our power and our might but by the Holy Spirit's. It is all for God's glory, not for the glory of humankind. You want to be expelled from the garden? Continue to walk in pride and arrogance. Continue to believe that you are a god worthy of praise and worship.

Our past is what makes us who we are today, whether good or bad. We can become what the past dictates we should become, or we can overcome. Our testimony can be a very effective weapon and a catalyst for someone else seeking salvation.

Mother encouraged me and all my brothers to drop out of high school. She didn't finish school, and neither did my father. I graduated and went to cosmetology school, but then I took a job at a bank, and from there I started my own business, which I ran for twenty-two years.

My brothers and I have all had difficulties coexisting with others because Mother told us the world was evil. We grew up paranoid. All five of us had to force ourselves to eat out in restaurants or go to movies, and when we did so, it was painful. Over time you overcome if you refuse to give up. I remember my first date was to a fast-food restaurant and then to a movie, but I couldn't eat. I was very awkward and felt like everyone was watching me.

We come to the Lord just as we are. He knew us before He called us in. We can blame Mother until we die for our years of misery, but that only exalts the enemy. God gets the *W* in my life!

MERCY

For all the blows that have landed
To cause a cut or a bruise;

For the curses created by hateful words,
Relationships abused;

For all the evil thinking,
The envy to nourish, the lust for the drinking.

It was every man for himself while the ship was sinking.

Promises were made but never kept.
We were stealing for feeling, but we never wept.

Have you been redeemed?
Has your house been healed and cleaned?

Pay forward the life so graciously given.

Mercy's not earned; it's peace for the living.

Discernment is Key

I have known Christians who are in a close relationship with the Lord and who are used in the gifts but who marry someone or go into business with people who are deceivers, liars, and cheats.

A Christian should be able to recognize the snakes and dragons, but we don't always do so. We are human and prone to making mistakes or to following our hearts, which can be deceiving. Love and lust can be confused for each other, and both are very powerful tools of the enemy. You should be able to trust the people who are close to you, like your parents, your spouse, and other relatives. Unfortunately, many of us have snakes and dragons inside that circle of trust.

People both within the church and without have criticized me for cutting off all contact with my mother, but they are not the ones who have to deal with her. In order to remain sane, I could not communicate with my mother on a regular basis.

I was molested by a family member at the age of nine. That was the first and last time it happened. I was a small girl, but I had four brothers, so I knew how to defend myself. I became very aware of my surroundings from that day forward. One thing that bothers me about that incident is that I went from being an A student to a C and D student. I could not get that memory tucked back into my brain for several years, and it affected my attention span. My mind was taken over by that horrible moment. As my grades dropped, I started feeling like I was stupid, just like Mother had said.

I just sold my private-duty home-care agency after twenty-two years of being in business. Maybe I wasn't totally hopeless after all.

THE FRUIT AND THE TREE

I have three children. The first day alone with my oldest, my son, I wanted to take a shower. I panicked and called my mom to ask her what I should do. She told me to take a shower and to quit being so stupid. I pulled the cradle next to the bathroom door and left the door open, thinking I would be able to hear my infant son if he fussed. He was sound asleep and slept through the entire shower.

I would practice lying back in the recliner putting him on my chest, and then I would wrap my arms around him. Hugging doesn't come natural to me. I was afraid that I wouldn't love my son, because whereas Mother showered my oldest brother with love and affection, she never had any for me.

Do you ever say you are not going to be like your parents? I was definitely not going to be like my mother. If I was lucky enough to have a daughter, I would love her and tell her she was pretty and smart and that she could do anything she put her mind to do. I would buy her beautiful clothes and encourage her in everything she did. I swore that I would be a good mother and that my daughter would know that she was loved and wanted.

What I write in *Where Are the Heroes?* is my opinion and expresses the way that I saw my life and my relationship with my mother. I am very sure that if she were writing this book, it would sound altogether different.

Buffalo is the nickname I use for my mother. When I was little, I had dreams about my mom. In the dreams, her head would get enormous and take on the image of a big black buffalo. In truth, my mother is only about five feet tall, but her rage was huge.

When you are a small child, the person or persons in authority over you are larger than life. Rage can make someone seem much larger than they really are. Even as an adult, my fear caused my body to shake and my teeth to chatter when I heard Mother's voice on the phone. It was about eight years after my salvation that I was set free from that fear. As previously mentioned, I was thirty-seven when I got saved.

When Mother would call or I would see her, she would start the conversation by reminding me that she was my mother. She would tell me how much she desired to know my children. I tried to talk to her calmly, but my insides trembled so hard I sounded like I was shivering. She would jump right into the past, saying how awful my dad was, how horrid his wife was, and how much she hated all of my sisters-in-law, past and present. She would praise the grandchildren she loved and curse the ones she hated. *Hate* may seem like a strong word, but it is a word she used frequently. Mother used lies and money to create chasms between her family members, and demanded loyalty from the ones she could manipulate.

One time Mother called me when I was in a mall shopping with my daughters. She was crying or pretending to cry (I couldn't tell). She briefly told me that she desired a relationship with me and asked if I would come to see her. I agreed and went to see her the next day. This was our pattern every few years. The first thing Mother said to me was, "Oh dear, you're getting fat." The second thing she said was that I was looking old and that I should take better care of myself, because my good-looking husband was going to find someone younger and prettier than I. It had been nearly five years since our last visit, when she had given me a similar warning.

Mother asked if I had brought pictures of my kids. I had. My youngest was one and a half years old when my mom had last seen my children. They are now thirty-two, twenty-seven, and twenty-six. I gave her high school photos of the kids, and the first thing she said was that my son was just as handsome as his dad. She started reminiscing about taking him shopping when he was seven years old. That was the last time she'd seen him. She thought my oldest daughter was beautiful. When she got to the picture of my youngest, she made a face and asked me why she was so fat! I could have climbed over the table and slapped her rude mouth. Instead, I talked about all of my daughter's attributes and wouldn't let Mother ask any more questions about my kids.

Mother loved my son and would take him shopping and buy him bags of clothes without even considering the girls. She used to do the same thing to me. She would bring home bags of new clothes for my brothers and tell me it was important for them to have new clothes because they were boys. She would reluctantly take me to the This and That Shop, which was a used clothing store. I have nothing against used clothing, but this was in the sixties and early seventies, when people gave clothes away because they were worn out. Mother would tell me that she couldn't shop with me because I didn't like the things she liked and we would end up fighting. She was right. We tried shopping together a couple of times, but I always wound up crying in the store because she would berate me in front of other people. I always felt defeated and hopeless. We just didn't mesh. Besides, she didn't enjoy spending time with me, a point she had made very clear. "It is for your own good" was the resounding excuse for her cruelty.

Children are like puppies; they are loyal to, and desire affirmation and affection from, their parents. They come back again and again, even after a beating, with the hope that this time things will be different. *This is going to be the day that my mother gets the revelation. This will be the day that she sees me as a blessing and not a curse.*

That never happened. My mother described my infancy and childhood as some of the worst days of her life. "You bawled all the time" is what she often told me. My father has told me that he would come home from work and hear me crying in the crib. He would check on me, to find I was soaked and dirty. He had no idea how long I'd been there. He said that my mother would hold me up over the bed and drop me in to take my breath away in the hopes that I would stop crying. She also held my head under cold running water to shut me up.

My mother would tell me when I was just a little girl that she had told God she didn't want a girl. She came to the conclusion that God was punishing her. She always told me that she never wanted me. She was never pleased with me. I still remember being in my room alone, folding my hands and closing my eyes, and praying, "Oh God, oh God, if you are real, please get me out of here. God, if you are real, please find me another family."

START THE CONVERSATION

———◆———

When was the last time you talked to God? Do you remember? Was it when you were desperate or hurt? in want or in need? He doesn't care how long it has been, as long as you start a conversation with Him and talk on a regular basis. Do you feel close to God or communicate with Him, the Holy Spirit?

I am God's church, and you are the church if you believe that Jesus is Lord. I know that I am saved, because I can tell you the day, the year, what time of day it was, and what I was doing when I was saved. Much like Paul, I was on the road to somewhere. I was crying and telling God that I was sick of myself and of my life. Suddenly, I felt His hand rest on my left shoulder and He spoke to me. He called me "dear daughter." He went on to ask me what He could do for me. I heard Him as well as I hear anyone else speaking to me. I know now that I was hearing from my spirit, but in that moment His voice seemed audible.

My dad never stood up to my mother, so I grew up with an opinion that most men were either weak or evil predators. On the day I was saved, I felt love in its truest form, and I knew that I could trust God.

> He is provision and protection.
> He is Redeemer and King.
> He is wisdom, knowledge, discernment, revelation.
> He is peace, joy, love, forgiveness.
> He is Deliverer and conviction.
> He is the first and the last, the beginning and the end.
> He is creator of all things.
> He is *faith*.
> He is joy and peace.

You are my morning star.
You are my sunny day.
You are the cleansing rain and the morning dew.
You are the wind and the waves, a mighty force.
You are the thunder and lightning, the antiseptic.
You are the reason that I live.
You are to be praised.
You are to be adored.
You are worship.
You are grace.
You are mercy.
You are life.
You are *hope.*
You are my friend.

I trust You.
I need You.
I love You, Lord.

Born in Sin

W̶e are born inherently sinners, which means that we are not little gods and Jesus is not already in us. We are created in God's image, but even as children we are focused on ourselves. We learn to depend on people to provide for us and to protect us. It doesn't matter whether you were a nice person growing up; you still have a sinful nature. Every person must be born again by repenting and asking Jesus for salvation. In order to be saved, you must believe that Jesus is the Christ who was fully God yet walked on this earth as a man.

I was saved, but I still had the lying spirit in me for a year. I refrained from lying during that year because the Holy Spirit had made a home in me. Some have argued that God will not share a house with a demon or that at the moment of salvation we are set completely free from sin. However, some things do come out after much fasting and prayer. I know that this is a biblical truth. I also know it is truth because it happened to me.

The day I was born again, I was given a Bible and I started reading. The Word came alive to me. I started in the book of John, as had been suggested to me. I read night and day. My husband would get up at two or three in the morning to check on me because I would sleep a little and just have the need to read or to feed on the Word of God. The Lord knew me. He knew that in order for me to understand what I was about to go through, I was going to have to fight, I would need my sword—the Word—and I would need to have the Word firmly planted in me.

When Jesus faced off with Satan in the desert, He was not tempted. Jesus responded quickly with the Word of Truth, our sword. How do you respond when you are faced with temptation?

PRAY TODAY

Pray today like it's the last.
Read the Word and even fast.

For those you love or want to hate,
Pray and don't debate.

The day is getting late.

For every hour holds the power
Of salvation,

A celebration of new creation.

Obey the Spirit, not the soul.

It is God who makes you whole.

Faith and Obedience

I want to share a testimony with you concerning prayer and obedience. God can pray through any Christian at any time if the Christian is in tune and in fellowship with Him. We were created to be His hands, His feet, and His voice.

I picked my children up from school every day. Of course they are all in their twenties and thirties now, so this was fifteen or sixteen years ago. We always took the same route home, with the exception of just one day. On that day, we took the long route. I don't remember why.

We were approaching the intersection where I intended to turn left to go home when we noticed an ambulance, a fire truck, and several police cars. As we got closer, we realized there had been an accident. I recognized the car, but it was nose down and tail up, leaning against a boulder in a yard. I read the plates and I knew that my son's friend drove that car. We had to turn around and head for home, taking our regular route. I felt my stomach contracting even before I got turned around. It was gonna be a long night.

When we got home, I could not stand still. Pictures were flashing in my mind. I had to find out which kid had been driving that car. No one knew anything about it. When my son got home from practice, he was shocked to hear about the accident. However, he did know that it was his friend's younger sister who was driving the car.

The contractions in my stomach were getting stronger, so I went to my closet. I got on the floor and asked God to fill me with the Holy Spirit, to use me if He wanted, giving Him full rein over me. I began to pray in the Spirit, and very quickly pictures began to flood my mind. I saw two girls with blonde hair. Both had head injuries and broken bones. Both girls were in a deep sleep.

I went to battle not knowing who the second girl could be. I went to bed around 11:00 p.m., only to be awakened by the sound of a slamming door (God's signal for me) at 3:00 a.m. I continued praying. I went to my prayer chair and asked God to fill me with the Holy Spirit again and to use me in whatever way He wanted, again giving Him full rein. I became still before the Lord and waited for a vision or a word.

I got a picture of a girl with shoulder-length blonde hair lying on an operating table. God allowed me to smell her hair, which was full of blood. I know this sounds strange, but it really happened. I could smell the blood in her hair, and I could see her although I did not recognize her. I saw her head and neck braced with a halo for support, so I knew her neck had been broken. God then led me down through the body, showing me broken ribs, a broken arm, and a broken pelvis. I also saw that surgery was taking place. I just prayed for the girl's life and for the life of the driver. I saw both girls in a deep sleep, but my main focus was on the passenger.

My husband got up around 4:00 a.m. to check on me. I described to him some of what God was showing me. He could tell I was in the zone. This kind of thing happened a lot in our house, so he was getting used to it, although he didn't fully understand it. However, my husband did recognize that it was God.

The next morning my son came down and said that he had gotten a call from a friend who reported that there were two girls in the vehicle at the time of the crash. Both girls were in a coma, but just one had been in surgery earlier that morning, having her spleen removed. My husband was a bit shaken because I had described to him the things God had been showing me at 4:00 and it was matching up with what we were now being told.

We don't always have to be thumping our Bibles. God knows how to reveal His power, majesty, and glory to your family. If we are faithful, He will be faithful.

The girl on the operating table was having her spleen removed as I was praying. I had never met the girl, but God revealed her blonde hair to me, and my son confirmed that she did have blonde hair. I will refer to her as Passenger.

The driver came out of her coma first and was released from the hospital after a time, but she required therapy at home. Passenger did not come out of her coma for several more weeks. I was moved to pray and to travail nearly every day with Lynn, who would come over. She and I would spend time in worship, waiting on the Lord to guide us.

After several weeks, there was talk about unplugging Passenger's life support. I was devastated to say the least. Passenger had eight doctors, and only one was against this. I was told that the priest was counseling the parents to let her go. Were they wrong? No, they were looking at the situation with their limited sight and understanding. According to the professionals, the situation was hopeless.

The decision to discontinue life support just caused me to fight that much harder. I knew beyond the shadow of a doubt that God did not waste my time. I knew that I had seen the Lord whispering in the girl's ear while she was sleeping. He kept asking Passenger if she wanted to stay or go, saying that it was her choice. People say that those in a coma can hear you. I believe that. But I also know that the Holy Spirit can be heard by a mind that seems to be asleep as well.

Family and friends went to work preparing a goodbye service on that Sunday night. I had attended every Sunday night service to pray for Passenger's healing. I took my son to the goodbye service and sat in the back of the church, as I always had. It was horrible to sit among those grieving while knowing that this girl was not going to die. I wanted to get up and scream when they were playing it's-been-nice-to-know-ya music and everyone was claiming her death before she had even died! Monday morning was pull-the-plug morning. Everyone accepted the limitations of humankind over the healing power of God when now was the time to fight!

Our ride home was very quiet but for my son's sniffles. He was eighteen, and I had hardly seen him express his emotions. When I pulled into the garage, he was crying, which broke my heart. I asked him how well he knew Passenger, and he said, "I just can't believe I will never see her again," which indicated that he knew her well. I took a deep breath. Becoming defiant, I grabbed my son's hand. I reminded him of what God had shown me and of the hours and days God had used me to fast and pray for the girl. I told him that God never wasted time like that if He intended to take someone from the earth. I then asked him if he would be in agreement with me if I prayed for Passenger. He said yes.

I prayed: "Father, I pray for all truth to be revealed in the name of

Jesus. I pray, Father, that You will send a rescue, and confirmation that [Passenger] is not dead. I thank You for this life and for the fact that it will not be wasted but used to build Your kingdom. Lord, give my son peace tonight, and build his faith in You, not in the doctors or the world, but in You. In Jesus's name, I pray all things. Amen."

Monday morning came. One of Passenger's doctors convinced her parents to leave her life support on because the medications she was on would make it seem like she had no brain function. They did what he asked, and today she is alive and well. She went on to school and is now married. I have never met Passenger, but I did see her once at a school function after she had been released from the hospital.

We know nothing apart from God.

EAT, DRINK, AND COMMUNICATE

M uch prayer is birthed out of desperation and selfishness, although
I believe that God wants to hear from us no matter what is on our
minds. Any communication is an open door for God to bless you. Do you
ever ask God what He wants? Do you ever tell Him that you would like
to give your day to Him and that you will try to obey Him if He makes
himself clear to you? None of us know when we are going home to be
with God but every day is an opportunity to obey.

People, especially young people, spend hours listening to negative,
violent, depressing music. The demons roam around looking for weak
and depressed people so as to make them weaker and more depressed.
The goal is to get you to focus so much on yourself and on what you
don't have that you consider taking your own life. Demons fold you
up into a tight blanket of depression and self-pity until you surrender
to hopelessness. It is like drowning. And the pain is real. Self-pity is a
slippery slope.

Feeding on the Word, drinking in the Holy Spirit, and communing
with God every day is very refreshing and encourages a thankful heart
and a charitable attitude.

WHO'S YOUR GUIDE?

We can multiply the fish and the loaves.
We can feed the hungry in droves.

Why aren't we?

We can cast out demons,
Pray for the lost,
And heal the sick,
But what is the cost?

Can you walk on water?

Do you have a gimmick?
Do you have a clue?

Whom are you listening to?

Is the Holy Spirit guiding you?

INTERCESSION AND CONFESSION

Prayer can be silent, noisy, loud, painful, exuberant, anointing, discerning, prophetic, revelatory, or knowledgeable, or an exercise, a warning, an encouragement, a correction, or a source of direction. Prayer can be done on your knees, on your belly, while standing, while sitting, when in a squatting position, while walking, while sleeping, in your closet or car, or during church or an event, and can happen anytime, day or night. The Holy Spirit calls, but it is up to us to respond.

God wants us to be open to the moving of the Holy Spirit. God will never put on a show at your expense. I have been led to leave a room at times when God needed to use me to travail and at times that have gotten loud with moaning and groaning from my inner person. Travail is taking on the pain and suffering of someone else. Most often sin is simply a symptom of something much deeper. It takes a move of the Spirit to flush it out. Someone who intercedes for others simply sees the source of pain or sin, pulls that closer to the surface, and fights or wrestles to push the truth out in front, until the person is free.

I was saved, baptized in the Holy Ghost, and was speaking in tongues as well as seeing prophetically while God was preparing me for deliverance. I have had pastors and evangelists tell me that what I report in my testimony is impossible. Nothing is impossible for God. We are all unique, and only God knows how to prepare someone for deliverance. Many get saved and wind up in the same place or somewhere worse within a year or two. Why? No one is finishing the job; there is no follow-through.

When we come to Christ, we come just as we are. Some who come late to the party may have more baggage than others. We all grow up in a unique home with unique circumstances and with our own generational crud. At the moment of salvation, our sins are forgiven, but that is just the beginning. It is not the complete package.

When a person goes to the altar or comes to you personally, it is because the Holy Spirit is drawing them. There is conviction, maybe confusion, maybe torment, that is the driving force behind the seeker. Please do not ask the person to repeat your generalized prayer of repentance for salvation. Repeating the Sinner's Prayer is your words, not theirs. Every person needs to face God with their own words of repentance and desperation. Each person needs to humble themselves before the Lord and ask to be saved. If they are crying, tell them to fight, to push through, and most importantly to be honest with God. It is the breaking point in spirit and in truth that will drive the person right into God's arms.

Listen, telling folks that the angels are partying in heaven because they just repeated something you said is to tell them a lie. Repentance and deliverance are personal, and the invitation to Jesus is personal. When you choose to surrender your life, you are allowing some exposure and putting yourself in a vulnerable position. But at that point it shouldn't matter, because you are tired of the torment and of pretending.

As we grow in righteousness and He sees that He can trust us with little, He will test us with more. In other words, when you learn to see and hear in the spirit, when you recognize that it is God and you obey Him, He will use you even more to bring forth His will.

THE INTERCESSOR

A mind that's filled with worship
All the night and day
Will stir the spirit into battle.

To pray without delay,

Turn down the noise
And turn off the toys.
It's time for us to fight.

Oh God, there's so much darkness.
Please shine Your mighty light.

Prayer is given flight.

Anticipate;
Don't hesitate.
Don't look back to see.

Stand your ground and celebrate
The Spirit's victory.

The prayers that go beyond this realm
Are the arrows Satan fears.

With the Holy Spirit at the helm,
The beast is brought to tears.

THE SLAMMING DOOR

I awake to the sound of a slamming door. I get up, and then I wake my husband to check the house. The sound is so loud that I believe someone is breaking in. This was happening as much as a year prior to my salvation. I know now that God was trying to get my attention. It reminds me of 1 Samuel 3.

After my salvation, I continued to hear the slamming door between 3:00 and 4:00 a.m., so I shared this with my new pastor. He told me that it wasn't unusual for God to use the sound of a slamming door to wake the intercessor. He gave me a tiny book written by Kenneth Hagen called *The Intercessor.* There it was in black and white, proof that I was not crazy!

I got into the habit of getting up, grabbing my Bible, a pen, and some paper, and retreating to the living room to greet God. I typically close my eyes and relax, waiting for the Holy Spirit to lead me. I ask the Holy Spirit to shut out all noise or distraction so that I might hear Him clearly. Typically I see moving words or pictures, or I hear God speak to my spirit. He rarely uses more than one to three words when giving me direction.

On one particular morning my belly was full of words! I hadn't realized how frustrated and discouraged I had become. Very quickly words began to rush to the surface. I started to write. At first I was rambling, but around the fifth page I was beginning to feel the frustration break away. I felt the weight of my errors, presumptions, bitterness, and disenchantment lift. Within a few weeks everything that came to my mind was in the form of a rhyme. I wasn't trying to come up with poetic messages; they came to me. Just like anyone else, I have had some frustration with church. Some of the poems reflect that, but they also reflect my love for the Lord and the church. God has planted a seed of desperation in me for the body of Christ, His church, His bride.

We live in a day when Christians practice righteous indignation in place of righteous living. I rarely meet a group of Christians without coming across those who avoid reading the Bible because they do not have time or they do not understand it. Many churchgoing people live together outside of marriage, drink alcohol on a regular basis, swear, smoke, and lie. Divorce is at an all-time high among Christians. Adultery is common. Perversion sings from the altar of God and then treats the youth to ice cream.

We worry more about community gossip than about spiritual power and sanctification. Is it all good? Should we agree to disagree?

UNITY

Let's agree to disagree.
Round and round we go.

Wait in line to catch a flea,
Serving to and fro.

How can there be unity
When no one's in the know?

I cannot figure for the life of me
How worship becomes a show.

Does anybody know?

How do you get to heaven when you're still attached to earth?
How do you get born again when your mother gave you birth?
How can you be rich when your bank balance marks your worth?

Do you know when to spank and when to spare the rod?

How do you tell your friends that it's Jesus you applaud?

How do you walk in the Spirit when you depend upon your feet?
How do you tell God that you'd really like to meet?

Prayer Warrior

I saw the movie *War Room* with my dear friend Jill. She is definitely a prayer warrior, one who sees and hears in the spirit. When I met Jill, she was very sweet but not a warrior. She desired the "more" that I desired, so she put all her effort into her relationship with the Lord. Today she is such a benefit to the kingdom and lays down her right to sleep, to eat, and to rest in order to pray for others whenever she is given an assignment.

Prayer is the job of every Christian. There are many ways for a Christian to pray. One can pray aloud with words or within one's mind. God can read your mind. One can pray in tongues; with moaning and groaning as with travail; through weeping; by making a declaration or prophesy; through worship in spirit and truth; through music as with an instrument; by dancing; by reading the Word; or in repentance or thanksgiving. Any conversation with God is prayer.

If you do not know how to pray, consider saying the following to God: "Lord, teach me how to pray. Your kingdom come Your will be done, O God. Holy Spirit, impart to me Your wisdom, revelation, knowledge, and discernment in every situation. I don't know how to pray as I ought to, so, Lord, pray through me by the power of Your Holy Spirit."

The heart of any church or fellowship is the prayer team. The prayer team should consist of seasoned warriors and of all those who feel the need to intercede but who may not yet understand travail and intercession. There should be teaching, encouragement, and leadership in every prayer meeting. Prayer night is not the night for competition or jealousy. Leaders need to deal with issues, not cater to the flesh. The enemy will use hurt feelings, emotions, envy, and gossip to tear down a powerful prayer ministry.

Proverbs 14:30 reads, "A heart at peace gives life to the body, but envy rots the bones."

The prayer group doesn't have to look or sound lovely, but it must be unified spiritually. It will probably be the most diverse group in your fellowship. Leadership leads by assigning tasks, recognizing needs, and teaching, disciplining, correcting, and unifying the team. We all need to understand the role of the Holy Spirit—the Source. The Lord gives every good leader the tools he or she needs: patience, grace, humility, and the desire to see others grow. God will choose men or women who are known to be full of the Holy Spirit and who operate in the spiritual gifts.

I had wonderful leaders when I became a part of my first prayer team. It was a husband and wife team, and the husband was an elder. I took many of their Sunday school classes as well and found them to be authentic Christians. God uses people who are seasoned to help us along, but He wants us to learn from Him directly as well. The goal of God is that we learn to hear His voice and to distinguish that voice from all others. He desires our obedience so that He can accomplish His will through us and for us.

It is good to acknowledge and respect leadership; however, people are fallible. Because of this, we need to know the Word and stay filled with the Holy Spirit, so that we can discern and recognize false or wrong teaching and preaching.

I still have great respect and much love for that couple although I no longer attend their church. They knew me and respected the gifts in me. They allowed me room to grow and to fail, and encouraged me to follow the leading of the Spirit. Ministry continues even when we lose contact with someone. The example and knowledge I gained through them and from the way they live their lives continues to teach me, to remind me, and to hold me accountable.

A leader produces leaders. A controller produces followers and admirers.

WILL YOU REMEMBER ME?

Will you remember me when I'm gone?

Did I ever sing you a song?
I hope not.

How did we get along?
Did we speak in passing or share a glance?
Did I welcome you into my home, by chance?

Did I fix you a meal or make you a deal?
Did I offer you tea or ask how you feel?

Did I give you my coat or lend you a dime?
Did I rush you out or spend some time?

Did you feel His love when I was around?

When you were with me, whom did you see,

Him or me?

Two Are Better Than One

As I mentioned earlier, I had a prayer partner for ten years whose name was Lynn. She was about ten years older than I. I remember being in a prayer group with her. She prayed in tongues very loud. I was a new Christian and learning to hear from the Holy Spirit, so I was distracted by it. I started praying for God to quiet her down.

Lynn and I were called to a mutual friend's house to pray with her. We were outside on the picnic table. Before we started, I began praying in my mind for God to please keep Lynn quiet so I could pray. I continued to pray silently until I faintly heard, "Be still and listen." I heard it three times—three times—and I knew I needed to listen. As Lynn prayed in tongues, I listened. I began to ask with my mind for the ability to "see" what Lynn was praying. I did. I saw a stream with rocks in it, and the water was flowing at a steady slow pace. I also saw green grass on the banks with nice healthy trees. I then began to see words floating on top of the water as they made their way across the rocks and through the turns. The same sentences kept going by, so I knew it was God.

I got very excited. I told Lynn that God had allowed me to read what she was praying. I also confessed to her what I had been praying for previously, and she forgave me for it. We began meeting at least three or four times a week to pray together.

Lynn died one morning while sitting in her recliner, reading the Word. I was undone for a long time afterward.

Lynn usually got up, studied for a bit, and prayed. On this particular morning, she was waiting for her little granddaughter to show up. She said that she would call me after Liv arrived so we could share what God was communicating to each of us. This morning Jen, Lynn's daughter, called me and asked me to come out because she couldn't get her mom to respond to her. I knew. Lynn lived about three miles from me, so it didn't take me long to get there. I walked in and there she sat. I lost it for a minute or two, asking her what I was going to do without her. I wailed like a wounded animal. When they came to take her away, I went to her prayer room. I realized that God had been trying to prepare me for this. Just a month prior to her death, Lynn was riding along with me on a job. On the way home, she asked me if I would make sure her family would play the song "The Galilean" at her funeral. I told her that I didn't want to talk about something that wasn't going to happen for a long time. She told me to promise. I got a little angry and asked her why we were talking about her funeral! She calmly said again, "Would you please make sure they play it? And I would like for your brother to sing it."

I told her that I would, not realizing how little time I had left with her. I was very happy to know about the song, and I wished I had been more sensitive about something she was giving a lot of thought to.

Do You Know Me?

Am I a muffled voice in the crowd,
Singing out loud just to be heard?

Are my prayers of the flesh, or are they hitting the mark?
Are they reaching your heart?

Am I lovely or loving just to be seen,
Or am I really mean?

Does my time or my timing have anything to do with You?
Do I have a clue?

Do You recognize my face?
Is there any trace of Your amazing grace?

Change me today.

I need to know that what I sow
Is for You,

Only for You.

Serve In Obedience

We live in a day and age where everything seems to be about *feelings*. I am not a person who cares about being politically correct. It is the truth that sets us free, not making people feel better about their sins. As a Christian, my job is not to judge the world and its standards. However, I do live in this world and am concerned about the condition of things. Don't get me wrong, I am not surprised at what is going on; I am just concerned.

If you have studied the book of Revelation, you shouldn't be surprised that our nation is in the state that it's in at this time. We are called to pray for our leaders, not only those in the church but also the ones over our towns, counties, and states, and those in government. Whether you like the party in office or not, as a Christian your job is to pray for God's will to be done. It doesn't matter how you pray or how well you pray. Just pray!

Prayer is a conversation even when it is silent. You can pray with your mind, because God can read your mind (whereas the enemy cannot). When I don't know how to pray or what to pray for, I do pray in tongues, seeking God for answers. My prayer language is not always the same, but it is always used for the same purpose. The Bible tells me it is the language of angels.

It is not my business to know all the details of a situation. God may desire to keep some things hidden from us for the sake of the person receiving ministry. When we pray in our prayer language, we are communicating with the heavens on a different level. I don't know the depth of my own heartaches the way God does, let alone those of a stranger or an acquaintance. And just because God has decided to keep some things from me doesn't mean that I can't effectively pray.

God has used me in prophecy over the years. I have been surprised at how most Christians view the prophetic. I have had people come up and ask me what I see in them. I say that I see nothing, as I am not a psychic, adding, "Unless you asked me to pray for you, God would not make your business my business."

I did not go to college, so when the Holy Spirit called me to serve in the college and career age group, I was terrified. I was one of two volunteers to show up, but I was the only one who stayed. Imagine that. I had planned to take a break because I had been serving in the women's ministry for three years. When I tried to leave church on the morning when we were to pick a place to serve, I could not get out the door. I would walk back into the hallway, where I would be drawn to the college sign. I told God that it couldn't be right, because those kids would chew me up and spit me out! But I went. It was crazy in that tiny room. These young people were not as polite as the women had been.

I was accepted and stayed for three years. It was fun. At the end of the three years, God began to give me a vision of leaving. I had the same vision for weeks, over and over, so I knew. The day I woke up with the interpretation, I told the leaders it was time for me to go. God had planted me there, and then He moved me on. It is all about His will and His desires for the church and for me. I am a Christian in training. When He can trust me with a little, there will be more to come. The ministries we serve in are not ours. If we never get out of the way, then others will not have the opportunity to serve.

I had so much fun with the young adults, and I found out that they wanted the truth. They wanted to *know* and to be used by God. I don't care how old people are, most of them want to know that there are boundaries, rules, restrictions, and order. Kids, even at the college level, know that if you use discipline and correction with them, it means you care. We all need to know that someone cares. Love is the key, even when it hurts, to changing hearts. *Love* is a strong word and shouldn't be used loosely. Love is power. Love can give life, change an opinion, change a situation, change an attitude, and change a mind. Love draws a person to Christ, but it is repentance that saves. Love shines the light on our sinful nature and causes a reaction.

I have listened to people share testimony with a motive to impress. When God calls you to share your testimony, it is to give Him glory. His power, evidenced through a miraculous deliverance, breeds hope.

People go to Christian college and learn how to deliver a five-point sermon, but how many learn to hear from or to obey the Holy Spirit?

Will you stop service or skip reading the announcements one morning to give room for the Spirit of God to move? He just needs for us to create an atmosphere of praise and worship in spirit and in truth and to teach from the Word. He will do the rest. I used to love to show up to church half an hour early on Sunday and go into the sanctuary with worship music playing just to worship and pray.

ACTING

Acting, fact-ing, worship the mind,
Souls in control leading the blind.

A little here,
A little there;
A little eases all despair.

Just one bite into the devil's lair.

If I die today, who will care?

Stories bought as lies are sold.
The church is polite, while the devil is bold.

This scene is getting old.

MY PRAYER LANGUAGE

Today there are church attendees who discount Jesus as just a good man and a good example to follow. Some believe that we already have Jesus inside of us at natural birth and we simply need to wake him. All this nonsense is confusing but not surprising. The world is already deceived, and Christians are being deceived through the church.

I was saved while driving. I was broken and telling God that I could no longer live like I had been living. I told Him that if He was real, then I needed to be saved. I felt His hand rest on my left shoulder. It was heavy enough to feel, but it was light and gentle at the same time. I looked up at the clouds. They were moving really fast in both directions, like they were parting. I was driving but wasn't aware that I was driving at this time. I heard a voice say, "Dear daughter." It was soft. I felt like love was washing all over me. He then said, "What can I do for you?" Sobbing, I told Him that I didn't want to drink anymore, that I didn't want to cuss like I had been, and that I wanted to be a good wife and mother. Within seconds I felt like I had lost one hundred pounds. Suddenly I was aware that I was driving. There were no other cars around. I was a crying mess exploding with joy. I had felt love, pure love, for the first time. I started laughing and crying, both at the same time.

I had been with my brother all that day. He was newly saved. I had seen something real in him, and I wanted it. He had peace for the first time. Prior to being saved, I felt that reading the Bible was like reading a language foreign to me, but my brother gave me a Bible when I left that day and I started reading it. The lights had come on. My blind eyes had been open. I could read and understand the Bible! Now if Jesus was the one living inside of me, why hadn't I been able to understand the Bible before? Furthermore, if it was Jesus who was living inside of me from birth, then why would I ever commit sin? Why had my brother looked different, sounded different, and behaved so differently if something different hadn't happened to him?

I continued to attend church with my family, and I continued to read the Bible. During Mass I wanted to stand up and shout to everyone that God was real and that I had been saved. I wanted to clap and dance and tell everyone all the ways God had already healed me. The Holy Spirit had moved in and I had been changed.

Getting baptized in the Holy Spirit and praying in tongues was natural for me. I didn't ask anyone about it. I had read enough to know that it was important, so I asked God to baptize me with His Holy Spirit and fire. I held my arms up one day and told God that I wanted everything the Bible said that I could have. Because I had heard God in my car, I knew He could hear me, so I talked to Him all the time. I am not exaggerating when I say I read the Word for hours day and night for the first two years after my salvation. I was absorbing it like a sponge and understanding it. I talk with God about everything all the time, and I pray and sing in tongues even while I am vacuuming.

The apostle Paul prayed in tongues a lot. It is something he encouraged for building us up in the spirit. When I pray in my heavenly language, I get words and visions from the Lord that help individuals as well as the church. I asked to be baptized in the Holy Ghost, but I didn't pray in tongues right away. I was cooking spaghetti and praying for my mother when I stopped and said, "I don't know how to pray for her anymore, Lord." When I opened my mouth to say something else, I was praying in tongues.

I don't know all there is to know about my mother or why she saw me the way she did. I don't know what is in anyone's heart, but God does. The Spirit of God will pray through us for things we have no understanding of or insight into. Some things are painful or unthinkable and may cause us to pray with our emotions when God simply needs a vessel to bring forth His will. God responds to the depth, the desperation, and the holy desire. We don't know the depth of pain or disappointment, not even in our own hearts, because we are good at burying our skeletons and hiding, lying, and faking our way through life. It is the Truth that sets us free, and Jesus is the Truth, the Word of God.

Be Careful

Be careful with your eyes and what they see.
Pornography can be a stinging bee.
Set the windows of your soul
On things that make you whole.

Be careful with your ears and what they hear.
Idle words can sow the seed of fear.
Turn down the sound or walk away.
Make the most of every day.

Be careful with the tongue and what you say.
Don't deceive or try to lead the innocent astray.
For every one you turn from God, there will be a price to pay.

Be careful with your feet and where they go.
Don't go running to the biggest "holy show."
Revival isn't planned by man.
Fire burns wherever He can.

Be careful with your mind and what you know.
Good and evil toss you to and fro.
Knowledge can be a trap to thee, affecting your integrity.

So be careful.
A price was paid, but not by you.
It certainly wasn't free.
A holy heart stood in your place.

Religion
Nailed Him to a tree.

He died *just* for you,
Just for me.

Intimacy In Worship

Worship is a form of communication, something we were born to do. Worship strengthens our relationship with God and renews the mind. Worship is another way to pray.

I believe that Song of Songs is difficult for many to understand because of the mind. We need to ask the Holy Ghost to lead us through this book of love and intimacy in spirit and in truth. When you read Song of Songs, pray for your mind to be sound and for the ability to see this book as Christ would have you to see it. I have heard worship leaders giggle and talk about how sexual the book is. Song of Songs is about intimacy and freedom. It is about trust, the most profound trust. Song of Songs goes beyond our flesh and gives us a deeper understanding of love, unlimited joy, and tender mercies. It is where deep cries out to deep and where to die with Christ is preferred. Song of Songs is meant to take you to a place in love that no person can fill. His desire is to satisfy your thirst and hunger beyond food and water or fleshly desire. That which is fully given is fully received.

God is not perverse, and love is not sex. There is a place in all of us that God longs to touch because that's where we see Him for who He really is. It is where we see our reflection when we look into His eyes and know that His heart is a father's heart and a husband's heart. It is where we hear Him call to us, "Beloved." This is where we feel the fire in His hands as He touches our spirit to heal, to deliver, and to restore us, to make our mind sound. Sex is meant to be enjoyed between husband and wife, but it is a brief moment of intimacy between two people. The deeper you look into the eyes and the heart of God, the more you realize how fleeting all things of the flesh are. He is forever. He is the deep crying out for you, and He calls you in.

WORSHIP

A worship song is not a sing-along.

The Holy Spirit is not a ride-along.

What's in your heart?
Who's on your mind?

What is it you're looking to find?

I Want It All

---◆---

I typically keep my eyes closed during the worship service so as not to be distracted. Occasionally the Holy Spirit will have me pray for someone. I don't ask questions; I just begin to pray in tongues quietly. Worship is between me and God. It is a time for me to clean house and to express love. Only God sees the deepest part of the heart. Every moment, whether you are in church service, driving in your car, or doing laundry, is an opportunity to pray and worship. You can pray with your words, spiritual words, your mind, or through travail (moaning and groaning). All communication with God is prayer, and He is listening.

There are so many wonderful Christians who do not believe in the baptism of the Holy Spirit or are fearful of it. How do you operate in the spirit or become spiritual without receiving the spiritual anointing from God? How do you work for someone you barely know? No one has to be baptized in the Holy Spirit or pray in tongues, but how do you communicate in the spirit? How do you live in the spirit?

I have been rebuked on this topic more than I have on any other, and it is discouraging. I have had people tell me that praying in tongues is not biblically sanctioned today and that it was a gift given only to the disciples. There are preachers who preach this to their congregations, and they are hindering the spiritual growth of many. Are pastors afraid of losing control of their sheep? Are pastors taught to discourage the church from becoming spiritual?

I desire everything God has for me. I asked to be baptized in the Holy Spirit without hesitation. I was all in. God knows how to give good gifts to His children. I trust Him. Which of you, if your child asked for a fish, would give him a stone? What do you think God is going to do to you if you ask for His anointing or the gifts of the Spirit? Do you think He would punish you? Is it fear that keeps you at a distance?

I had no one feeding me religious doctrine or explaining the rules to me. For two years it was Him and me, disciple and Teacher, consuming the Word. I have never put walls around God for my comfort, because I want to live this life to the fullest and to serve Him. I desire close communication with the Holy Spirit. And when I worship God with my spirit, there is power and I am changed.

Lock onto God during worship, forget everything around you, and start talking to Him, wooing Him, and admiring Him. I tell Him good morning and say that I love and trust Him. I say, "It's just You and me, Lord, just You and me." Behind my closed eyes I begin looking for signs of Him. And I listen. When God sees that your heart is locked in, adoring only Him, He will speak to you in a way that you will understand.

I see bright colors during worship. The closer He comes, the more brilliant the red gets. My whole self is relaxed and carefree and I am joyfully convicted. I get shivers thinking about it. God gets to the deepest parts of us so that we can be made whole.

It is important for a worship team to be prayerful, and respectful toward God and each other. A person who leads worship needs to be held accountable, as this is the individual who is responsible for ushering in the Holy Ghost and setting the spiritual atmosphere. Whatever is going on in any leader is liable to flow out or to spill onto the people they are ministering to. Demonic activity happens lawfully inside our churches. Ignoring it will not make it go away. Making light of sin helps no one and can bring down an entire house. When a leader is spiritually weak and living in blatant unconfessed sin, the sheep are in danger. Sin gains access to the church through people, and if it isn't dealt with, it will destroy the credibility of the church and the ministry.

Worship is a time for the Holy Spirit to go through the room touching hearts and minds, gently convicting, creating an atmosphere of repentance. This is not a time to be politically correct or fearful. Nor is it a time to watch the clock. This is the time to allow God to reign over the sanctuary, to change us, to heal us, and to restore us. Deliverance can be ugly and it can be noisy, so this would be a good time for the pastor to actually teach!

Repentance is a sweet-smelling sacrifice to God. As you burn that sin at the altar, God and the angels rejoice!

I know there are nutty people out there who want to bark and cluck and do all sorts of crazy things to draw attention to themselves. Stop them. Tell them to sit down and be still. If they leave and never return, so what? Your job is to protect your sheep and your house. God bless them. We have got to stop being so fearful of the spiritual that we silence the Holy Spirit. We definitely have to stop fighting about Him. If you don't want more, don't ask for more, but do not keep others from seeking more. If you hinder anyone, you will be held responsible.

RAIN

Listen for the rain.

Wash me.
Redeem me.
Relieve me of this pain.

God, let it rain.

There's no more room for sadness
When God sits on the throne.

He mutes the voice of madness.
With Him you're not alone.

There is no year of Jubilee,
For all the years are His.

All we do is serve, and see
That He is who He says He is.

STUDY THE WORD

Have you been around people who seem to have the "inside scoop" on God? They talk differently, respond in peace, and know how to bless others. When they serve, they seem happy to do it. They seem to have time to help, and they seem to have money whenever there is a need. They are very encouraging, and their prayers seem to get answered.

Proverbs 14:30 reads, "A heart at peace gives life to the body, but envy rots the bones."

I enjoy dissecting each word of a certain scripture to give me a broader understanding of what God is trying to tell me. I simply use my dictionary and pray for the Holy Spirit to pull it all together for me.

Heart: the central, vital, or main part; core; the center of emotions, personality, attributes, etc.; mood; feeling, spirit, courage; one's innermost nature.

Peace: freedom from war; agreement; calm; quiet; freedom from conflict; silence.

Rest: to enter His rest; sleep; relief from stress or distress; the repose of death; absence of motion; silence; to refresh; cease work; to be at ease.

Content: to be satisfied in all situations.

Content: meaning or substance; all that is contained in something.

Body: the whole physical substance of a person; a group or unit; richness, consistency, density.

Envy: discontent or ill will over another's advantages, possessions, etc.; a desire for something someone else has—covetousness.

Rot: to decompose, decay, spoil, ruin.

Bones: structure, foundation, base; hard tissue forming the skeleton of most vertebrates.

The heart feeds the body and keeps it going. All blood goes through the heart, where it is filtered and then redistributed through the head and body. When the heart is healthy, the body functions well and has a strong defense. We need a balance to operate or function properly and in good health.

The heart of the body of Christ is made up by the prayer warriors, the intercessors, and those who travail. Prayer and prophecy breathe life into the body, protect and defend the body, expose the body, and call out for repentance, obedience, reconciliation, restoration, spiritual unity, and maturity. A true prayer warrior listens for God's direction and watches for a vision or for movement in the spirit. Obedience is key to bringing forth God's will and the outcome that will bring Him glory and honor. Arrogance, pride, and the lying spirit remain a constant threat to God's church.

DECEPTION OR THE HOLY GHOST?

On one occasion, while he was eating with them, he gave them this command: 'Do not leave Jerusalem, but wait for the gift my Father promised, which you have heard me speak about. For John baptized with water, but in a few days you will be baptized with the Holy Spirit. (Acts 1:4)

> But you will receive power when the Holy Spirit comes "on" you; and you will be my witnesses in Jerusalem, and in all Judea and Samaria, and to the ends of the earth." (Acts 1:8)

> Now, Lord, consider their threats and enable your servants to speak your word with great boldness. Stretch out your hand to heal and perform miraculous signs and wonders through the name of your holy servant Jesus. (Acts 4:29)

> After they prayed, the place where they were meeting was shaken and they were all filled with the Holy Spirit and spoke the word of God boldly. (Acts 4:31)

The disciples were dependent upon the Holy Spirit. They knew Jesus, and they knew who the Holy Spirit was: God.

I have listened to many preachers, teachers, prophets, and evangelists. It isn't hard to discern which ones are anointed by the Holy Spirit and which ones are speaking through their own minds. I have sat through meetings where there was much hoopla and no real moving of the spirit. I witnessed a prophet speaking false words into a man I knew and encouraging him, when I knew good and well the person being spoken to was full of demons. I also knew the person had been giving a lot of money to the church, so it felt like the prophet was priming the pump, as opposed to helping this person find freedom. I have witnessed countless youths and adults falling down, as opposed to being slain in the spirit. This, sadly, has become a sport, and I for one am sick of it. I have been slain three times in twenty years, and I can tell you exactly what God did with me while He had me in a surrendered position. He isn't about the show. If we don't stop this nonsense, He will get on with the show, but we may not like it. God is not to be made a mockery of. Exalting human beings and causing our focus to be on humankind is why Lucifer fell. It is why Eve bit the fruit and why Adam followed. It is why an entire generation of Israelites did not make it into the Promised Land.

The Holy Ghost is working to free us from self, or pride and arrogance. When a pastor steps up to the podium to deliver a message from God and hasn't even asked for God's help, he is in grave danger. There is coming a time, very soon, when such men will be removed from their positions because they have no power to bring real change to someone's life. The power comes from the Word of God and through the anointing of the Holy Spirit, and when a person is in obedience to the Holy Spirit.

Acts 5:32 reads, "We are witnesses of these things, and so is the Holy Spirit, whom God has given to those who obey him." If you jump up to verse 29, you will see that Peter is telling the spiritual leaders as well as the lawmakers that they must obey God rather than humankind. (These people were being persecuted for preaching about Jesus.)

John 14:25 reads, "All this I have spoken while still with you. But the Advocate, the Holy Spirit, whom the Father will send in my name, will teach you all things and will remind you of everything I have said to you."

The Holy Spirit is God with us. The promise of God walking with us once again and talking with us through His Spirit is very exciting. He is our Counselor and Teacher. When we are loyal to study His Word, our understanding is increased, and so is our faith. It should be forever growing. The Word is new seed every time we read. The Holy Spirit waters that seed, and it keeps growing inside us until it becomes who we are.

In times of ministry, the Word just bubbles up in me. I cannot memorize, and I had trouble in school because I would forget what I had just read and I would freeze during a test. With the Word I simply have to be faithful to read, to study, and to seek understanding from Him. He does the rest. It is not about my mind retaining; it is about my heart receiving while my mind is being renewed. It is the washing of my mind with the Word of God.

Jesus is the bread of life. If Jesus is the bread, then the Word is also the bread, because He is the Word. When we eat this bread, the Word of God, we are fed to full with wisdom, revelation, knowledge, discernment, and love—in other words, Jesus's character! So the Word of God washes us (renews our minds) and feeds us (gives us strategy and knowledge), and with it we are trained to use our weapons (prayer and a sharp sword) against the spiritual enemy. Just like any soldier, we too must go through boot camp. When Jesus was in the desert, He certainly was never tempted. Jesus knew His enemy, and when the enemy tried to tempt Jesus, His reply was always to quote the Word—the Truth.

John 15:26 reads; "When the Advocate comes, whom I will send to you from the Father—the Spirit of truth who goes out from the Father— he will testify about me."

The Spirit of truth should be *in* us. To use exaggeration is to lie. Lying is never okay. I was shocked to find that some leaders lie to avoid hurting someone's feelings or to keep them from leaving the fellowship. I have come to the conclusion that a portion of God's church operates much like the government. It tells you what you want to hear to keep the money flowing and the kingdom growing. Who is this kingdom for?

LIAR

A liar's heart from the start.

Born in sin, we begin.

A child's tale is called a fib.
Lying is funny from the crib.

Children see and children do
Exactly what we tell them to.

Generations from old to new,
The lying spirit will follow you.

Teach
That exaggeration is a breach
Of integrity and holy speech.

Repent.

Give God his place,
So that all disgrace will be erased.

Who's on the Throne?

It is never my desire to offend people. That being said, I know that I am not the only person who sees the church today as a weakened vessel. Fortunately, there are several spots around the world where God has held His position, where Jesus remains Lord, and where the Holy Spirit has the lead. Unfortunately, there are far more churches or places of fellowship where humankind is on the throne, leadership is lord, and the plans and schemes of human beings are producing weak worship, weak sheep, deep debt, sin, flattery, entertainment, lifeless, powerless messages, numbers without depth, and the blind leading the blind.

God is the I Am.

You can quote the Bible all day long, but are you living the Word? Are you a reflection of Jesus before others?

If you feel down or depressed, worship God. Nothing brings more joy and cleansing than when we are focused on Him. When you draw near to God, He reveals all truth. Only He knows what's keeping distance between us and Him. There is power in the Word and power in the worship. Responding to God is like pouring drain cleaner down your sink. The clog is pushed through and the water flows freely. It is the job of the Holy Spirit to deliver us as we work out our salvation with fear and trembling. Many times our wounds are self-inflicted, our needs are merely desires, and our aches and pains are emotional. Until you walk in the righteousness prescribed by God, you will go round and round your mountains, getting nowhere.

I have heard it said that if you are still repenting, you do not understand grace and mercy. No one is perfect, not even one. When I came to the Lord, I needed immediate relief and I got it. However, over the years I have been through times of deliverance, some more powerful than others, depending on how strong the hold was or how tight I was holding on to the things that were holding me back. The enemy cannot read our minds or our hearts, but God can. The Holy Spirit searches us out and heals, redeems, edifies, delivers, and sanctifies us.

To be sanctified means to be set apart for salvation.

To be edified means to be corrected, directed, and encouraged to live a more righteous life.

I don't want to be looking into the eyes of my Savior and have Him say, "Depart from Me; I never knew you." Many will say, "We cast out demons and healed the sick in Jesus's name," when in reality they were performing to gain fame and glory for themselves. Obedience is how we love God. You can do many good things for humankind, but what is God telling you to do?

We live in a world where people *expect* the government to take care of them, where people *expect* the church to take care of them, and where adults *expect* their elderly parents to continue to take care of them. This becomes a generational cycle. Even Christians *expect* God to fulfill their every desire, whether good or bad, but they ignore the Spirit over and over, day after day, passing by the Bible to turn on the TV.

The Word of God tells us to control the flesh, to put the desires of the flesh under the control of the spirit, yet we don't. I'm speaking about myself here too. The Word tells us to take responsibility for our behavior, our emotions, our own lives, our children, our jobs, our finances, and our church, but we stand with our hands out (not up) during worship with our minds full of lustful, unhealthy desire and greed! Repentance stirs the heart of God and He shows mercy. Grace gives us time to adjust to the truth.

Fight that your mind be sound and that you have in mind the things of Christ. Pray for others and get your focus off yourself for a change. God may bring your healing or deliverance in the midst of your unselfishly battling for someone else.

We need to lose the self-pity and the follow-the-leader mentality and get spiritually right. We need to lose the idea that we have to be just right before we can do anything for God. God will use the humble to confound the wise. I have found that as I am ministering to others, God is taking care of my business. I don't usually bring Him a list of my wants, needs, and desires. He already knows them. I ask what I can do for Him today, and I try to obey. When my heart is right toward Him, I can trust that He will take care of me.

TRADING IN ...

Conviction for comfort,

The truth for a lie,

Integrity for fame,

Faith for the game.

Which church has the best name?

There's the powerless,
Cowardice,
The meek, and humble pie,

The rigid,
The workers,
And those who preach a lie.

All they see are dollar signs when they look into your eyes.

Does it make you wanna cry?

It should.

THE ANOINTING

Matthew 16:21: "From that time on Jesus began to explain to his disciples that he must go to Jerusalem and suffer many things at the hands of the elders, the chief priests and the teachers of the law, and that he must be killed and on the third day be raised to life."

Matthew 16:22: "Peter took him aside and began to rebuke him. 'Never, Lord!' he said. 'This shall never happen to you!'"

Matthew 16:23: "Jesus turned and said to Peter, 'Get behind me, Satan! You are a stumbling block to me; you do not have in mind the concerns of God, but merely human concerns.'"

Peter loved Jesus but was still lacking discernment. Peter was saved but had not been baptized in the Holy Spirit. Peter flew off the handle many times, allowing his natural instinct to determine his response. Peter was not yet a spiritual man. God defies logic and overrides intellect.

Jesus told His disciples to wait after His ascension, when they would receive the promised Holy Spirit, the gift, the anointing by fire, before continuing the ministry without Him.

The disciples had not become apostles and were not yet equipped to carry on Jesus's ministry. They were saved but still students. The disciples had learned from Jesus, but they had not yet been anointed by God. Many people excited about being a Christian skip their training and go headlong into ministry. Many never receive the anointing from God to move in the spirit; they simply try to accomplish God's will through their own flesh and understanding.

The apostles made reference to being baptized in the Holy Spirit many times, differentiating between that and repenting and being baptized in water. They encouraged many to be baptized in the Holy Spirit. When church leaders today teach that the gifts of the spirit ended with the apostles and were just for that time, I say, "Read your Bible!" Paul, in Corinth, preached vehemently about the spiritual gifts, and especially prophesy and praying in tongues, so Paul didn't keep it to himself, did he? He encouraged all to ask for and to receive the baptism of the Holy Spirit and to prophesy, but also to act with propriety.

Asking God to baptize you with His Holy Spirit and fire is asking God for His anointing. Many who "do" ministry without the anointing wind up burning out quickly. They lack joy and peace, they rarely experience miracles in their ministry, and ministry for them becomes stagnant. Most people don't even bother to ask the Holy Spirit what ministry, if any, they should be a part of. Many leaders don't care; they just need a warm body, with a clean background check, to serve. When we don't ask God to lead us into ministry, whom are we serving? Many serve because they thrive on the praise of human beings. Many need to be doing ministry but begin complaining about how worn out they are. God may have someone who is actually anointed for or in training for exactly that area. Do we ask God to show us who, when, or where?

It is the same with prayer. God may put someone on your mind or in your spirit, but you try to ignore it in order to get to your list of needs and requests in. After all, you only have so much time, right?

When someone is in my vision or on my mind, I try to stop and pray right then. I lift them up, put them before God, and ask God to show me the need and how to pray for that need. I thank Him for using me to pray. And if nothing comes to mind, I ask God to bless the person and to cover him or her with His protection and love today.

When someone calls with an issue, I pray right there and then on the phone. I am afraid I will get off the phone, get on with my day, and forget to pray. God can remind me, yes, but again, how many times do we ignore God's prompting throughout the day?

Many spiritual warriors sit idle in the church or at home because Christians are afraid. Christians fear the Holy Spirit (God), yet they will practice magic, yoga, reiki, witchcraft, necromancy, divination, idolatry, and adulation. Many Christians are liars, thieves, murderers, perverts, and abusers being led by evil spirits, yet they fear the Holy Spirit (God). In Christian homes you can find pornography, violence, demonic symbolism and entertainment, drunkenness, and drug addiction, but say the words "Holy Ghost" and fear comes over the whole house.

Many shepherds are busy tending to community affairs and church building, leaving the sheep to fend for themselves. The wolves are busy keeping the weak sheep sick, hungry, and disillusioned. The church becomes anemic.

Telling someone that God has a plan or a great plan for their lives is true but also deceiving. Most people skip over the part where you have to surrender your whole self to Him and go through spiritual training, including study of the Word. How about the part where you are no longer to control your own life but to be led by the Holy Spirit, your life becoming a life of obedience? How about telling new converts that this life is not about them at all but about God and His will. How about telling newborn Christians the truth, and that this life in Christ is challenging but wonderful, that the miracle of watching someone surrender themselves to Christ or gaining freedom from a demonic stronghold is way better than any other thing happening on the planet?

It is fun to serve the Lord! It is fun to be used by God. Yes, it can be hard, but just like giving birth to children, when the pain is over there is new life and new potential, fresh hope and peace. There is restored joy, and He leaves you wanting more.

You will find that as you serve Him, your needs are met with more than enough. Father knows how to give good gifts to His obedient children, to His loving, adoring children. He does not withhold any good thing from those who obey Him. Change can hurt a bit and confession can be humiliating, but isn't that what you came to church for, a change?

The old serpent is having a party watching us tear each other up, preaching watered-down sermons, counting the attendees instead of the newly saved, keeping peace, relating our words or language to the world, and even stripping the Holy Bible of God's authority and legitimacy.

All denominations think they know the truth when it comes to the Holy Spirit. Some acknowledge Him, some allow the Spirit to move, some try to manipulate and emulate a move of the Spirit, and some preach vehemently against anything they do not, will not, or cannot understand. I have witnessed too many evangelists, prophets, and pastors push people down, encouraging a fake response to prayer and sensationalizing or exaggerating their services to gain fame.

Speaking in tongues is a divisive issue. It is a spiritual function. Unless you have some understanding of it, you may see it as weird or scary. Mercy on the pastor who avoids this subject because he does not understand it.

The Holy Spirit is where my help comes from.

What is the balance? What is real? I would say the real deal is in your own home, in your own heart, when you are alone with God. Maybe for you it is in your car worshipping or in your small group where you can be real about God. When you have a true relationship with the Lord, people see it, hear it, and know it.

My encouragement is that you go to church and fight for the truth. Fight for the real deal and stop following the leader. Get involved with what the leadership is doing, and get to know the elders. Make sure your fellowship is operating biblically, but most importantly, make sure you know your Bible. Many leaders want people to serve without knowing the spiritual temperature of individual peoples. Many who serve are worn out because they are in the wrong position or else are trying to do everything, leaving no room for others to serve. If God has called you to a particular ministry or has positioned you as a leader, you will have His peace. If you are trying to control, or impress, or take on responsibility that is not yours to take on, you will be worn out, overbooked, overcooked, stressed, and burned out. If your church is short on volunteers, maybe you have too many programs.

Fearing the Holy Ghost is like saying you fear food. Just as you cannot live and function without food, a Christian cannot live and function in obedience to God without acknowledging the Holy Spirit. His kingdom is coming and His will is going to be done, whether through you or someone else. God will make the rocks cry out or cause a donkey to speak if necessary.

How did the serpent gain access to the garden? God desires our devotion, love, affection, and obedience. Adam and Eve were expected to trust God, to obey God, to respect the limitations God has put upon them, and to discern evil. The serpent was allowed in the garden, so I wonder if he only had access to that tree or if he was free to roam around. I believe that he had access to the tree of the knowledge of good and evil but was given boundaries. Humankind had dominion over the garden, but until human beings opened the door to evil, evil couldn't cross the threshold.

It seems to me that today's Christian wants to have it all ways. God tells us that everything is for us but that not everything is good for us. God allows us to choose, but His desire is for us to choose the better, or more righteous, way. Can you discern good from evil? Do you know what God's definition of righteousness is?

SHAKE

Shake the heavens. Stir the earth.
Send fire.
The woman's giving birth.

Move the air with gale force.
Sound the trumpet from the north.

Do you see the rider on the horse?

Throw your lightning from the sky.
Burn through me so that I may die.
To live like this would be a lie.

I hear her cry.

The screams intensify.

Birthing pains; the time is right.
Perish, or find the light.

I will not give up this fight.

Cut the cord; remove the cast.
Throw it into the sea with all that's past.

Through His blood, I'm *free* at last!

WE HAVE ACCESS

I began writing poems and prophetic messages about five years ago when I was very ill. I woke up at 3:00 one morning, and instead of preparing for prayer, I listened as the Lord told me to write. Three surgeries later, and after a lot of time recovering, I have around two hundred poems/ messages.

God is speaking to the church just as He does through the Bible. The Holy Bible was written to draw the unsaved but also to raise up the saved, the church. The Bible is instruction, encouragement, discernment, knowledge, wisdom, revelation, God's standard, correction, direction, love, our compass, our training manual, and our atlas. The Word of God is Jesus.

The Word of God is a double-edged sword, and when that sword is wielded by an anointed servant of God, it convicts, draws, and then circumcises the heart of anyone who receives it. The Word of God is Jesus.

I would be up until dawn writing, and I got into the habit of snacking. I have gained thirty pounds, but I am determined to be free of this excess. I found comfort in food while battling pain and impatience.

God sees my heart, and He knows that I neither idolize food nor am addicted to it. I do, however, need His help in breaking the habit of eating at night. The following two poems are just a way to reveal my own weakness, ask for prayer, and throw in a little humor.

How fortunate are we that we have access to God through the Holy Spirit day and night, but also to Jesus through the Holy Bible? The heavenly realm is spiritual, and connecting to the spiritual is as simple as reading the Bible, praying, talking and listening, worshipping, repenting, expecting, loving, and desiring what's beyond the boundary.

SUGAR ADDICTION

Sugar! Give me sugar.
I think that I might faint.

No substitute will pacify.
It adds a deadly taint.

My head's in pain till I feed this brain.
My mood is that of Cain.

Sugar! Give me sugar,
Or I just may go insane.

BAD HABIT

I like eating chips in the middle of the night.

It's an urge that I don't fight.

I'm getting fat. What's wrong with that?
Who determines what size is right?

Chips are my comfort of all the foods.
Salty and crunchy, they change my moods.

I sneak a bag and then loosen the clip.
O the aroma. ... Do we have any dip?

Visions of Grandeur

------◆------◆------◆------

I had big plans and visions of grandeur when I got saved. I had one recurring vision of me on a platform with a microphone, sharing my glorious testimony before thousands of people. My testimony was so powerful that thousands fled to the altar for salvation. It took me awhile to figure out that we all have similar vision and that this new life is not about me.

God calls us to preach to the multitudes. Each person God puts in front of you is an opportunity to reach a multitude of people. When you are obedient to share Jesus with others, God honors that. You may not see your multitude here on earth, but I believe you will in heaven.

We are not to desire worship or adoration from others. Our job is to lead others into all truth so that they too will love the Lord. I did feel some rejection from family and friends at first because I left the family church, but I believe they were genuinely concerned. I have remained true, and at times I am overzealous, but they realize that I did not go off the deep end. I believe you can love the Lord enormously without turning people off. Again, it is not about you.

I had joined the family church to marry my husband. His dedication to going to church was one of the things that attracted me to him. I had an emptiness in me, and I believe God used that church as a catalyst for drawing me closer to Him. It was safe. I took classes with a priest, but I never heard him use the word *salvation*. My husband's family church was a starting point for me. I will never belittle it or see it as a bad thing, because God used it to teach me many things, including discipline. I believe that had I been born again while attending that church, I may have gotten more from it.

I attended Mass with my husband for about a year after my salvation. The Holy Spirit encouraged me to wait and discouraged me from asking to be released from the church. That was hard for me. I had visited a small fellowship a few times that was very different from Mass, and I really felt like it was a better fit for me, but I waited. One day after Mass, my husband looked at me and told me that he could see that I was not happy. He told me that if I wanted to go to another church, I could. We had always gone to Mass as a family and out to breakfast afterward, so I know this was not easy for him.

Simply by being obedient to the Lord and not insisting on having my way, God moved in my husband and allowed me the freedom to explore my faith. I soon found that my faith wasn't rooted in a fellowship or a building or a certain doctrine but in the Word and through the Holy Spirit.

So many Christians become infatuated with a preacher, a prophet, or an evangelist because they are infatuated with the power and boldness operating through such a person. The conduit for the Holy Ghost becomes the rock star, and Jesus becomes an afterthought. You can love Max Lucado and his books, but you can't make Max Lucado—or Joyce Meyer or Joel Osteen—your source for knowing God. And just because someone has a book on the best-seller list does not mean it is a book that is good for you.

I love Joyce Meyer, but she is simply a vessel for the Holy Spirit to operate through. She is not God. Joyce Meyer is an encouragement to me because she speaks truth with boldness and she knows the Holy Ghost intimately. Watchman Nee, whom I mentioned earlier, was held in a Chinese prison much of his life, so he knows well the power of the Holy Ghost and His sustaining power. He is gone from this life, but his teachings will go on forever because they are life.

People will disappoint us, even spiritual people, because we are not little gods and we are all a work in progress.

I pray before I read any book, including the Bible. I don't want to fill my head and my spirit with junk or confusion. I desire the truth. I want to honor God with my time and money, and I want to continue to grow in Christ. I rarely listen to secular music, because I want to stay in the attitude of worship. I pray in tongues even when I vacuum. These are just some of the things I do to stay in communion with God daily and to keep myself from being distracted by things that could muddy the waters or distract my mind.

I've been around women who have had unusual attachments to their pastors or other leaders. It is human nature to admire, and even to become infatuated, but it is never appropriate. Confession must happen so that this sin (yeast) will not grow and affect the whole church. You may need to get on your face before God and repent. The infatuation will eventually break and you will have peace. I would suggest reading a proverb daily and making that a habit.

There will always be problems and issues because we are people. Mercy loves through the pain, and grace allows time for healing and change. We must fast and pray for God's direction and timing. The goal is deliverance and restoration, which is important for the whole church.

You will not be victorious in battle unless you stand, face your enemy, and fight. Any Christian, even the most spiritual Christian, can open the door to demonic activity, even demonic control. I have seen it a number of times, and it is probably the most discouraging thing to me. Sin abounds in the house of God because there are few willing to deal with it or talk about it. Sin in the church is alarmingly common and rarely acknowledged. We pussyfoot around sin, treating it with kid gloves, as if it were a bomb waiting to go off. *It is!* And once it goes off, the entire assembly is affected.

Judge not lest you be judged. Boy, have I heard that enough times. When God speaks to you about someone and sin is revealed, that is God telling you that He is about to expose the situation. In my experience, He gives the person an opportunity to repent. When I am asked to deliver a message of repentance, it is followed by the blessing. One thing I do know is that if you are obedient to deliver the message, God will be quick in His action. His will is to restore, or else He wouldn't bother warning us. He will do all that He can to keep the infection from spreading, but He needs our cooperation. Some will run, but we must never give up interceding for them.

Keep this in mind: if you are prophetic and instructed by God to deliver unpleasant news, you will endure criticism, skepticism, and at times hateful rebuke. It comes with the job. The truth will be revealed sooner or later, and God, sending you before that happens, is giving the person the chance to avoid public humiliation. We are all sinners and we all fall short of the glory of God; read 1 Peter and 2 Peter. Remain humble, and love the church enough to endure the unpleasantness; it is not about you or your hurt feelings or feelings of rejection. The church is sick and in need of the truth. It is the job of the prophet to watch for and listen for any signs of the enemy. The prophet has more than likely been interceding, fasting, and praying for you for a good while. If they seem angry or judgmental, it could simply mean that they know the urgency of the situation and are trying to protect you.

There are consequences of sin. The enemy is like a ravenous wolf, seeking to devour souls and to destroy what God has built. Watchmen or prophets/intercessors must spend their time in prayer and training. Such a position can lead to an arrogant and prideful attitude and will kill the prophetic anointing faster than the lying spirit will. Our hearts must be so in love with God and His bride that we allow ourselves to be checked frequently.

Rejecting correction or direction makes you unteachable. You do not have to receive anything in the moment, but you must take all things to God for revelation. Be quick to repent and quick to apologize for a quick resolution if God is convicting you to do so. You will not have peace until you do. However, you are speaking for God, so you must deliver the message exactly the way He tells you to. You must not allow people to tell you what is appropriate to prophesy. Prophetic message is not subject to political correctness.

I am saved because God's mercy is more powerful than my sin. I am born again, but I have not arrived yet. My goal is to run this race and to reach the finish line: heaven. I pray that Jesus recognizes me. I am working out my salvation with fear and trembling because I believe the Word of God when it tells me that I could become worse off than before I was saved if I do not make my election sure.

You don't hear much of that preached in church anymore. The truth is watered down or turned into a comedic skit so that you will enjoy yourself enough to come back and tithe, and so that you won't feel uncomfortable or offended by the service. If you are comfortable enough, maybe you will join and become part of a team so that the church can wear you out serving a God whom you barely know.

I don't know where I fit. I feel like an oddball in church and out of church. I am odd around our mutual friends because I have nothing in common with them and I don't know how to make general conversation anymore. It is awkward and, I think, embarrassing for my husband as well, because the only hobby I have is Jesus. I just want to know Him more, and my only desire is to serve Him. I ache in my heart for the lost. We are never satisfied with our looks, our bodies, or our wallets, and we won't be satisfied until we know the Lord.

I don't talk the way I used to or make small talk, and I don't even know how to do it anymore. It is odd to me that when you bring up blessings and prayer, people feel uneasy, though I think I felt that way too before I got saved. If someone wanted to pray for me, I became very uncomfortable. People refer to me as religious, but I don't believe that I am religious at all. I am simply trying to live a spiritual life, in Christ.

When people talk about illness or injury, I want to stop and pray; however, I have to be careful not to sound like an alien. I realize that many people depend on their priest and preachers to do the praying and have either forgotten or were never told that we Christians are all called to pray, in the name of Jesus. We are called to lay hands on the sick and they will be healed, to cast out demons, and to preach and teach the Word of God so that people would come to repentance and be saved. It is not about us anymore but about the kingdom of God on this earth. Who is building up and who is tearing down? Do you know the difference?

Wake Up

Wake up, sleeper;
Rise from the dead.
Your bones are very dry.

Refresh yourself and look ahead:
Today's the day to die.

Wake up, sleeper.
Take His breath;
Revive the inner man.

Seek and search beyond this earth
For the Holy Spirit's plan.

It's not in the mind of man.

Understanding the Prophetic

We can talk a problem to death, but there is no power in that. Having faith expressed through prayer and living a life of expectation is what moves God. So many church gatherings become social and cease to be God honoring. We were meant to come together to pray, to worship God, to hear the Word, to repent, to be healed, and to surrender ourselves to God. People need to be set free from demonic stronghold inside the church as well as out.

I do not believe a lot of the junk I have been fed or that I have read since being saved. I read a little book called *Prophets Drive Me Crazy*. It was funny, I guess, but it really spoke to me when mentioning how people see prophets and when discussing how little people understand the prophetic ministry. I know that you cannot be a liar (exaggeration is a lie) and be prophetic. Nor can you be controlling and be prophetic. There are many false prophets who care more about being popular and positioned than about being obedient to God.

I don't know where people got the idea that prophecy is limited to positive affirmation and blessing. It is only a blessing if you heed God's warnings and then follow His instruction.

Don't believe everything you hear or every "prophetic word" that comes your way, but certainly check it with God and ask for confirmation from Him. This is what God desires from us. If we belong to Him, He will surely be quick to respond. Don't judge the prophet by his or her cover; simply tell the prophet that you will talk with God about the Word and expect confirmation. No true prophet would object.

A prophet can get a message wrong or have wrong timing, so grace is required, and sometimes crow will be served for dinner. Believe me, I have eaten a lot of crow!

I wasn't born prophetic; I was born again prophetic. This is not a gift of the flesh; it is a gift of the Spirit. Some try to control the message because, unfortunately, they fear humankind and believe that if they spare someone's feelings or leave out the uncomfortable part of the message, God will honor it.

SALVATION

Humility waters the trees.
Obedience comes in degrees.

Love will bring the mountains low.
Compassion flows with ease.

He moves.
I feel the breeze.
His breath renews the life in me.

Worship causes me to sway.
I'm dancing in surrender.

He whispers sweetly in my ear,
His voice
So kind, so tender.

Yes, dear daughter, surrender.

My light will shine through your inner man.
You'll rest beneath my wing.

You'll chase Me just to know my plan.
To Me your heart will sing.

O call on me, beloved. To you My everything.

WIND

Come, wind, stir up strife,
Like a spoiled child or a jealous wife.

Stagnant air to renew.
Send the rain; smell the dew.

Breathe new life; the bones are dry.
Pierce the darkness; light the eye.

Thunderous warning from the sky.
Seasons change.

We live and die.

Pastors, teachers, prophets, and preachers,
Expose the mold under your bleachers.

He sends the rain through the fire.
Thunder and lightning are His for hire.

Discernment is the key for you to see
Through acts and tricks,
Methodology.

The Word is God's decree.

Watch for signs and wonders.
Bend your weary knee,

For the lost the days are getting late,
So make your desperate plea.

Mind Your Own Business

M y husband asked me why I couldn't just go to church, pray, and mind my own business. He does not see the church as his business; God has not called him to that yet. It is difficult for me to be a part of something and not be used. I care about the condition of God's house, and I intend to obey God. This is not always a win-win situation for a prophetic person.

I was told by a pastor once that I only delivered negative words and correction to the church leadership. That wasn't completely true. God always gives me the promise for obedience as well as the warning. I understood where the pastor was coming from; I just wasn't sure what he wanted from a prophet.

I get frustrated when we do not hear testimonies on Sunday morning. We have evangelists, prophets, teachers, janitors, librarians, students, moms and dads, prayer warriors, and children sitting among us every week filled with life-changing testimonies, yet we get a brief time of worship, a five-point sermon, the bulletin, and maybe a skit or some other form of entertainment, and then we are done for the week. Are you satisfied with that? Are you changing or simply going through the motions?

Prior to my salvation, I had become an alcoholic and a foul-mouthed, bitter person. I was only thirty-seven years old. I had three children who were used to this behavior, because it was the "normal." My husband and I even drank at our children's birthday parties. I insisted on order and cleanliness, and I used that to cover the real mess that was me. We went to church every week, and our children attended a private school. I tried to stay slim, sport the right haircut, carry the right bag, and wear the right clothes. I tried drinking away the insecurities, but alcohol just made me more paranoid.

I tried playing golf like the other wives, but I felt guilty. I was leaving my children with a babysitter again, paying a babysitter again when we couldn't afford to. And there were so many things I could have been doing besides playing golf, drinking, and acting like a fool. My husband and I were members of the local country club, whether we could afford to be or not. I was from a small town and lived in the country. It may as well have been a foreign one! I never felt like I belonged. I tried to fit in by keeping up with the Joneses.

I couldn't do anything unless I was drunk. My husband and I would go to a wedding and I would need several drinks before I could dance or mingle freely. I had zero self-confidence. Our priorities were a mess. The day I got saved, I asked God to take the alcohol addiction away from me, and He did. Right there and then, the desire and need for alcohol was gone. My entire life changed that day, and I have never looked back. My mouth cleaned up without my having to try. I just wanted to love the Lord and honor Him from that day forward. I began reading a Bible my brother gave me. I couldn't put it down. I read for hours every day, and even through the night. I had time because I was recovering from a car accident I'd had the year before and I wasn't working.

I would talk to God all the time, even in the shower. God had spoken to me the day I got saved, so it seemed natural.

Worship touches God's heart and it changes us. When I spend time in my closet praying or in my living room dancing, or in my car, I am worshipping God and I become joyful. I feel His love for me when I am letting Him know how much I love and adore Him, how much I trust Him and expect Him to guide me, to comfort me, to provide for me, and to protect me. We were made to worship and to rely on God.

Lucifer, the most beautiful angel, was made to lead the worship in heaven, and we were made to fellowship with God and to worship Him here on earth. Unfortunately, like Lucifer, human beings want the praise and glory for themselves. It is in our nature. We are inherently sinners, every one of us. If we could change ourselves, redeem ourselves, we would not have needed a Savior. God loves us so much, much more than we deserve, that He came down to this miserable mess we've made to rescue us from ourselves.

God made us in His image and has emotions just like we do. We are given the ability to choose the direction we wish to move in because God wants us to choose Him of our own free will. God can change the heart and mind of a person, and He can change His own mind about a matter, but love is a choice and He is constantly vying for our attention. Love cannot be forced. This is greatly misunderstood, but in order to love God, He must be given unlimited access to our hearts and minds. He is love, and when the seed of pure love is deposited in us, we become love and a true reflection of Jesus. God has a will and a plan. It is my desire to be in His will, following His plan. I know change can hurt or be difficult, but when God changes us, He heals us—and the outcome is a renewed life filled with peace and hope, life everlasting.

A pastor told me once that we do not have free will if we are predestined by God to be a Christian. So what he was telling me was that some people are picked by God and some are rejected by Him. I rebuke this, as it is not God's will that any be lost. We are all born to worship God and to turn from sin. It is the job of a Christian to build God's church without prejudice. Does God know who will choose Him? I believe He does, but I also believe that we have until our last breath to turn to Jesus, and that He continually fights for our attention.

Job was used by God to bring about His will because He knew Job would remain faithful. The book of Job is a great lesson and a wonderful testimony of faithfulness. God knew that the heart of Judas was deceptive even after he'd lived with the disciples for so long. Judas heard the truth and walked with Jesus, yet he did not allow love to transform him. He was allowed to be part of the church, but he was a fake or phony. Another great lesson.

As Christian parents, we raise our children to know who Jesus is, and we encourage them to pray and to read the Bible. Our children may obey and even pray for salvation, but there will come a day when they will have questions about God. I believe that children can truly be saved, but many times they are caught up in Sunday school and the "stories" told to them by the adults they trust. We should teach the Word to children in a real way, not as cute stories. Children, in time, will think with a more mature mind and question their entire belief system. There comes a day when children must take responsibility for their own salvation. They need to grow up knowing that there are true heroes in the Bible and in this world. Soldiers, police officers, firefighters, missionaries, inventors, and other risk-takers deserve our respect.

Our children do not inherit salvation through us, but they are set apart and pursued by God through our salvation. This is why many pastors have trouble with their children. They have raised them in a Christian environment, taught them well, and assumed their salvation was real. It may very well have been real at the time, but as adults these children choose their own path in life. God will never leave them or forsake them, but they may leave Him. Children see the attention another child gets when they ask Jesus into their heart, and then they try to mimic the scenario for praise and attention or acceptance. It may not be real.

Everyone is predestined by God to be saved, but unfortunately we are born with original sin and must be washed by the blood of the Lamb. Jesus is our destination. Through Him we are saved and trained to live in obedience to God. The choice is ours. We are each given many opportunities in this life to surrender.

Church is not a club and should not take on the character of being a club. Church should be the one place where no one looks at your financial statement, the car you drive, the house you live in, or the clothes you wear to determine whether or not you belong.

Many people attend church out of fear out of obligation, or out of habit. Perhaps they are looking for hope and searching for love, and/or desiring change—or any combination of these things. Many attend because they are born again and have a desire to serve and to grow. Many, unfortunately, have been told that one has to attend church in order to go to heaven, as if going to church is all there is to it. I was once part of a religion whose law stated that if you missed church without receiving dispensation from a priest, you had committed a mortal sin, which meant you were going to hell.

I know lots of people who go to church faithfully and who serve faithfully. Some serve because their spouse signed them up or because they were asked by someone. Some serve because God anointed them to do so.

A prophet must prophesy, an evangelist must evangelize, and a teacher needs to teach. There are preachers and intercessors and so much more to God's body. Most anointed Christians operate in all the gifts or with some combination of the gifts as the Holy Spirit enables them. We are all called to serve the Lord, but not many are willing. When you are willing, God will send you and you will have peace. A true warrior is ready for anything in any situation and knows how to follow the leading of the Holy Spirit.

People go to church because it gives them hope of something beyond this life. They are searching. What are they finding in your fellowship?

God walked with Adam daily and talked with him, so why did Adam follow Eve? What would have happened if Elijah had followed all the other prophets because he feared for his life? He would have been killed right along with them. If Daniel had obeyed and worshipped the king, he would not have spent the night in the lions' den and the king would not have honored God. The first apostles followed Jesus and at times had to rebuke authority to do so. Esther sought God through fasting and prayer at the risk of her own life, and God rescued her nation. None of these people followed humankind; they all followed the leading of the Holy Spirit. We can be prompted by human beings and helped along by them, but we all need to hear and to obey the Lord first. Humankind's message should be a confirmation of what the Holy Spirit is already telling you.

I could go on with many accounts or examples of people being led by the Spirit, but if you don't read your Bible, you won't know for yourself anyway. I am not going to feed you all the scripture, because I want you to open the book and seek the truth. Dig for the hidden treasure—for you!

Go to church and be of help and allow the Holy Spirit to change you. Get your mind on the right thing and obey when God is trying to move you. Repent and be changed so that you can be used to help others. Being part of a fellowship is wonderful. Plus, we are called to operate in unity, to be of one mind and one spirit. That can be accomplished if the leadership is unified first. Whatever happens in the head affects the whole body. If the head is confused, then the body will also be confused.

When God speaks to you, it is from the spirit. Your gut feeling is not a premonition; it is the Holy Spirit trying to warn you or to give you knowledge and wisdom in a situation. You must be tuned in to God's Spirit in order to be familiar with how He communicates. When He is communicating with me, I see images or words running across my mind.

I feel things through my lower belly that give me caution or cause me to stop and pay attention.

To understand how God works through you personally, you have to have a relationship with Him. Simply talk to God. Talk with Him just like you would talk to me. Take your Bible and put it in your lap, tell Him that you desire to know Him better, ask him to have you open the Bible to the right page, to set your eyes on the right message, and to give you the understanding.

Why wouldn't He answer? It is His desire that we would seek Him and come to know His Word. The Holy Spirit is our comforter and our teacher. He leads us into the river, but we determine how deep we are willing to go. The more we seek, the more we will find.

God trains me in obedience in a number of ways, but the funniest way happens at the grocery store. Something like mustard will catch my eye; I may walk past it four or five times and leave the store without it, only to realize when I get home that I needed mustard. I had that gut feeling that I needed mustard. God is in the little things, but who is noticing? Are you listening to that still small voice?

I love the apostle Paul because he had not spent time with Jesus prior to His death or after His resurrection. On the road to Damascus, he "heard" the voice of the Lord. Now Paul, being a Pharisee, was zealous for his religion and his position in life. He was climbing the proverbial ladder, and people feared him and obeyed him. Paul was a man in authority and had achieved position in his religion. He was a cold, calculating murderer. He felt that what he was doing was protecting God and upholding God's law. Paul thought that killing those who preached freedom through Jesus was the right or righteous thing to do. I have come across many who are set in their religious ways who firmly and truly believe that what they are doing is righteous because it is tradition.

Why would God choose the likes of Paul to be His son? Why did He refer to me as His dear daughter?

There can be much pride and arrogance in a person or group of persons who feel called by God to a certain position. Most do not understand that every time God positions someone, it is yet another test of character, humility, endurance, righteousness. We go from glory to glory as we allow change. Change is necessary, and should be constant until we reach our destination. People in leadership tend to stay the same or suffer from burnout. Some fall into sin. These things happen because the ministry belongs to them. Self is now on the throne, and self is going to do great things "for" God.

I don't know how my husband kept from having me hospitalized after my salvation. I changed. I radically changed, and it was immediate. The first three days, I sweated like a pig, vomited off and on, and cried constantly. I was so happy though. I told my husband that it felt as if someone had lifted a ton off me. My brother gave me one of his Bibles to use until I got my own. As I've said, I couldn't put that book down. I had tried to read Bibles before, like the ones the Gideons leave in hotel rooms, but I could not understand a word of any of them. It was like trying to read a foreign language.

I still read the Word almost daily and find new and wonderful things in there. You have to dig for gold, and that is what the Word is, gold, hidden treasure. Your entire life should be devoted to digging for the gold.

SILENCE

Silence is a signal.
The beginning of a storm,
The smell of rain on the dusty earth,
Is nothing of the norm.

It's getting warm.

Call the ships that are out to sea quickly to the pier.

Wrestle with your fear.

I see the light as it hits the sky,
Showing me the way.
I stay the course as best I can,
But violence wants to play.

Will I see another day?

Only He can say.

I've nothing to lose.

Wash away my earthly fame;
Sanctify my core.
I don't want to stay the same.
With You I know there's more,

Much more.

GOD GETS ALL THE CREDIT

P aul tells us that for three years he was ministered to by the Holy Spirit and then he met some of the disciples who had walked with Jesus. Paul was very careful not to give any person credit for his transformation; instead he gave God all the glory and praise. God will use wonderful Christians to help us along or to spur us on toward Him. We are not to look to anyone as our final source, only God. People tend to be disappointing because we are fallible, whereas God is not.

I have been in some wonderful churches with wonderful people. I have been in some not so wonderful churches with wonderful people. I have been in wonderful churches that turned awful and awful churches that turned wonderful. I have met wonderful people who turned out to be not so wonderful, and not so wonderful people who became Jesus-loving, God-fearing, spiritual Christians. I sure miss fellowship when I'm not in it.

Just a Crutch

You say that He is just a crutch
For fools like me who are out of touch,

Hanging on to the dream of a bigger scheme.
A waste of time it would seem.

I've been called crazy and out of control,
Rebellious.
Judgment takes its toll,

Makes you want to hide in a hole.

Maybe I'm not called to be like you.
The snakes I see aren't in the zoo.

If you like the things that hide inside,
Keep them.
To thine self be true.

But let me leave you with a clue:

The eyes of God can see straight through
To the real you.

PAUL

Philippians 1 begins the way most of Paul's letters begin. He declares who he is in Christ, and he prays for the church and all the saints diligently. Paul calls himself and Timothy servants. Paul greets all Christians, elders, and deacons, not excluding any member of the body, and he blesses them from prison. He is spreading the gospel and spreading joy though he himself is in prison. He is not wasting time and is making the most of every opportunity. He is encouraging those God has entrusted him with so that they might understand and not be discouraged or afraid. He needs for them to carry on and continue in the Lord for the sake of the Lord and the church. Paul knew his mission.

In verse 9 Paul is praying for the church at Philippi to continue allowing the Holy Spirit to sanctify them, to change them through the Word, as they gain knowledge and discernment and become more righteous in the Lord. We must dig for spiritual knowledge and discernment. The flesh is limited, but the Holy Spirit (God) is unlimited and wants us to know as He knows, to see as He sees, to feel as He feels, and to love as He loves. Again, Paul isn't thinking of himself or his current situation. For him it is always about the church and God's will. Paul's salvation was so powerful and transforming that he never looked back. He is one of the most devoted apostles, not to mention the author of most of the New Testament. He caught fire and kept burning!

In verse 10 Paul says to discern what is best. He probably doesn't know whether he will live or die at this point, and he doesn't want his death to cause the church to disband out of fear. But in verse 12 we see that the captivity of the church at Philippi has actually caused the members to preach more fearlessly—and people are being changed because of it. Desperation for the church drove Paul no matter what his situation was. He feared spiritual chains more than the chains of humankind. Love for God was Paul's driving force.

I wonder, being in that circumstance, if I would be so gracious and thoughtful, or if I would be blaming God and cursing my salvation. Paul sees everything as an opportunity, because he knows that whatever happens to him is what God has allowed to happen. No matter how bad things get for Paul, he knows that God will make all things work together for his good. Paul didn't ask God to spare him or to relieve his pain; he was concerned for the church. Serving God is not about your comfort, your ministry, a building, the programs, health, wealth, or fun. However, it is fun and rewarding because He is God.

Jeremiah 29:11 reads, "'For I know the plans I have for you,' declares the Lord, 'plans to prosper you and not to harm you, plans to give you hope and a future.'" Again, I go to this scripture. If you know the Word and it is living in you, then you will lean on it and not on your own understanding. This is called faith.

A WORK IN PROGRESS

I have run from conflict many times, much like Jonah. I have not heard many positive sermons concerning the prophetic ministry and I feel that more people are taught to fear the prophetic rather than embrace it. I know there are kooks that pastors have to deal with but I have only been a Christian for twenty years and I am learning. I realize how little I know and understand but I also see how little most Christians know and understand the prophetic ministry.

I do not want to disrespect any leader and I do not want to be in rebellion, but I know when I am hearing from God and when He is speaking to me. I would rather a pastor get to know me and know my heart before judging me. I would rather a pastor volunteer to train me in spiritual propriety than to have one talk behind my back to other pastors about my weaknesses. This new life of mine was foreign to me; I needed help with it. I have been called a jezebel, a witch, a rebel, and a gossip. I have been all of these things at one time or another, prior to salvation, but I thank God that today I am His "dear daughter."

I have run because I have feared facing a pastor with another sin issue in the church. Being prophetic does not make you holier than anyone else. Indeed, when you see sin in someone else, it makes you very aware of your own shortcomings. It also makes you more compassionate and understanding, because you know what you yourself have been delivered of. Who am I to be giving such a message, and why on earth would God use someone like me to do it?

I believe that it is because I am willing to get up in the middle of the night or to spend an entire afternoon weeping and wailing for souls. It is not about me; it is about obedience and birthing God's will on the earth.

Several years ago I went through spiritual agony in light of a vision I was having. This vision came to me night or day and never changed. The characters in the vision were people I knew, loved, and admired. (I still do know, love, and admire them.) This was especially difficult for me because it involved the church leadership. So I ran.

I wound up at a revival meeting after months of being outside of church, and I was tormented. After the message was given, I went to the altar for prayer. The evangelist kept praying over others and pacing back and forth in front of me. I was repenting and was expecting God to really let me have it, to call me out as a false prophet. I was so fearful of humankind that I started second-guessing God's message and instruction, finally coming to my own conclusion that I was not in right standing with God. So the speaker finally came to me and led me all the way to the other side of the altar, where he started praying. Not only was he encouraging me, but I'd had the same message prayed over me just a week prior. At that time, I knew it was God speaking. This was confirmation.

I wasn't able to accept the prior message because I'd been expecting God to rebuke and punish me!

So when the speaker finished, I backed up and sat in the pew behind me. I did not know who was sitting to the left of me, but she slid over and whispered in my ear that she had a word for me but that it wasn't time to give it to me. I didn't dare look at her, because I was angry. I began talking to God about it because I knew He would not withhold from me. He does not torture us or torment us. The woman slid down to me again and whispered the same thing in my ear. I turned to look at her. I was really upset, so I am sure that it showed on my face. I realized, in that moment, who had been tormenting me: it was the wife of the evangelist who had just blessed me. So I looked up and said, "Okay, God, what is going on?"

It took just a second for God to nudge me toward the woman. I leaned in and said, "I need to get out of the belly of the big fish." She looked at me, surprised, and asked how I knew that was the message she had for me. I hadn't; I'd just done what God asked me to do, just like she had. She could have scooted right over to me and given me the Word from God the first time, but she didn't; she obeyed and she waited. God does not work within the walls of our belief or our faith. Obedience is the only acceptable thing.

This new friend then told me that she knew my friend Lynn who had died the year before. She said that God was showing her how deeply I was still grieving. She said that Lynn had passed her mantle on to me and that it was now my turn to pick up that mantle and teach. It was time to get on with it. If my new friend had not obeyed and waited for the Lord's timing, I may not have received from her. God's timing caused my heart to break. I could feel the depression and the mourning lift off of me.

It was time to shake off the self-pity.

ETERNITY

Time to live, time to die.

Time to laugh, time to cry.

Time to sing, time to pray.

Time to work, time to play.

Timing's key for you and me;
We must listen carefully.

The smallest voice can hold the key
To life beyond what we can see.

Eyes of the Prophet

You poke the eyes of the prophets.
Peace you guarantee.

You like the tickle in your ear,
But the truth you never see.

The only thing you tolerate is "unity."

Unity with what?
Don't dare to disagree.
Leadership has spoken;
They're the powers that be.

But this is what I see …

It is He who adds to the number when nothing's adding up.
He turns the heart of stone.

He takes the case of the hopeless cause
And builds Himself a home.

He moves a mountain from here to there.
He makes the oceans roar.

He whispers sweetly in our ear
And plants us near the shore—then tells us there is more.

THE HOLY SPIRIT

———————◆———————

The subject of the Holy Spirit and praying in tongues is a hot topic among leaders and the body. I don't know how anyone expects to be in unity if they eliminate the key to everything. The Holy Spirit teaches us all mysteries and opens up to us the secrets hidden in the Word. He comforts us if we let Him. Going through a tragedy of any kind can turn a world upside down. When that happens, this earthly world cannot give you inner peace; only God can, through His Spirit.

I don't know what the big deal is. I read about it in the Bible and asked God to baptize me with His Holy Spirit and fire. He did so. I didn't pray in tongues right away, but I kept hoping for and expecting it. I was praying for my mother while boiling noodles one day and I started crying. I looked up and told God that I did not know how to pray for her, but when I opened my mouth again, the new language came out. As I prayed in tongues, I began to get a picture of my mother. All I ever wanted was for my mother to love me. I had tried my whole life to get her approval, but there was no hope. God revealed her heart to me while I was standing at the stove. I wept out loud and I prayed with moaning and groaning for my mother's life. I was desperate, no longer for her approval, but for her salvation.

There are times when prayer becomes so intense that I have to get to the floor. There is a pulling in the lower belly that feels just like early contractions when a woman is preparing to give birth. God will use you to push through the issue just like you would in the delivery room. I know that sounds odd, because of course you're not having a baby, but you are fighting a battle for someone and you need to allow God to push through to the end for their sake, not yours. I believe many people have started to experience this and have stopped it out of fear or ignorance. Give God a chance and you will be used to travail for others, experiencing the hand of God at work in a very personal way.

Being used in the prophetic can be scary and confusing. It takes time for God to season and train a person, and the training starts with truth. For me, to allow God to bring up all the junk and hold it in front of me, only to erase it, was liberating. I didn't have to earn God's love, grace, and mercy. For me God's mercy was swift and His love was *big*!

Truth is the most basic character trait for the prophet. You must be truthful with God in all things, and you must speak the truth in love to others, especially if you are speaking for God. Listen, God can make a donkey talk if you refuse to speak for Him or if you try to distort or change His message.

A friend once told me that we grow by eating crow. She was very patient with me and taught me a lot about mercy. Mercy is not the absence of truth; it is the truth, in love. If you don't get that, then you are going to struggle and find yourself on the wrong side of God. You may be honored by your congregation, but you will not be pleasing to God and you will risk the removal of His anointing.

Prophecy is not telling people where to live or whom to marry. It is not about controlling anyone else's life in any way. What it is about is drawing people closer to God. The more we change or allow change, the closer to God we can become. Prophecy is spiritual, not psychological or mystical.

A prophet sees deeper than the flesh and bone, doing so only when God decides. The prophet is in constant battle, because the enemy does not want the truth to be revealed for fear a soul will be changed for good. A prophet may seem serious or loud or even angry, but again, they are battling for you. It can be intense, so have some mercy please.

While the leaders are chasing the prophets around trying to keep them under control, Jezebel is busy plotting the prophets' demise.

Where did we get the idea that God doesn't say mean or negative things and He gives us everything we desire? We don't have to repent anymore and it's okay to use some profanity or get drunk because the Word is old-fashioned, out of touch, and out of date, and it makes people uncomfortable. The Word is truth, powerful, convicting, and sharp! The Word is not the reason more people would rather stay home on Sunday; it's the unrighteousness, lack of discernment, lack of conviction, lukewarm sermons, and entertainment in church that turns people off. These things may be enticing at first, but they lose their luster over time.

God has a standard for putting people in position over His children. One standard is that these people are *known* to be full of the Holy Spirit and operating in spiritual gifts. They are also to be men or women of good character and in good standing with people who know them. This fight between the spiritual and the unspiritual church needs to stop! We are to be a spiritual people now, no longer conforming to the flesh. The flesh will not behave *until* you become spiritual. Do you know what spiritual means? It means not only having the Holy Spirit of God *in* you but also inviting Him to pour himself *on* you so that you might be fit to speak and to act on His behalf with courage and boldness.

In the Old Testament God put His Spirit on people like Elijah, Daniel, David, Jeremiah, and Job because He knew they would be faithful to Him. These heroes and others were not perfect, but they had their hearts set on God and His will.

We have the Holy Spirit (God) with us twenty-four hours a day, seven days a week. We have access like Adam did. We can talk to God and He will answer in ways we never dreamed. Being baptized in the Holy Spirit is for all who ask, but you must ask.

So many pastors, preachers, and teachers try to speak for God but do not have the Holy Spirit speaking *through* them. They bring lifeless, boring, dull stories to the altar, filling the audience with junk food, when the truth is right in front of them, the steak! Some try to entertain us by acting or joking around, trying to be funny, and then they wonder why people don't take their relationship with the Lord seriously. There is nothing wrong with humor, but we live in a very unpredictable environment where discernment and spiritual warfare are valuable assets to all Christians.

If you are prophetic, you can expect to deal with the Jezebel spirit. The jezebel has a close relationship with the pastor or his wife. She claims that everyone who has any objection to her is jealous of her. She holds herself in high esteem and considers herself a pastor of sorts. She loves controlling pretty much everything. Typically the Jezebel spirit surrounds herself with false prophets who allow her to control and interpret messages given to the church. She thrives on praise and will have you believing the fellowship would fold without her.

Pastors who silence or attempt to control the prophetic message will eventually feel a void, God's silence. Jezebel calls the shots, takes credit for the work of others, and feeds off praise and admiration. The Jezebel spirit can be in a man or in a woman.

So I'm Told

The dragon is bold.
Souls are being sold.

Wisdom is folly.
Murder is fun.
God is put on hold.

Deep in the heart you'll find no peace.
The flesh is turning cold.

Leaders are liars, and liars are good.
We butter our bread with mold.

Money's the honey and gossip is funny—so I'm told.

What Does a Prophet Look Like?

How does one become a prophet? What does a prophet look like? Paul tells us to pray to prophesy and to pray for the interpretation. The Holy Spirit decides who, when, and where.

I am a serious person who sees most everything in black and white. I wear a lot of black and white, I decorate my house in lots of black and white, and my color preference for a car is either black or white. Every friend that I have who is prophetic is a serious person and lives in mostly black and white as well. I have deep furrows in my brow, and I look only moderately happy, even when I am smiling.

I know that I need humor in my life. That is why I surround myself with people who make me laugh. I watch funny TV and I limit the movies I see, choosing either humorous films or something with a good message. I listen to worship or God-honoring music, and I decorate with things that make me smile or stir conversation. I love dogs, which I believe are a gift from God. Plus, they are the perfect example of unconditional love and devotion.

The prophetic gift and anointing are given by the Holy Spirit. A prophet is transformed by the Word, worship, repentance, and obedience, just like every other Christian who desires a close relationship with God. By trial and error is how we learn anything, and forgiving ourselves is part of that. Humility, courage, and faith in God are requirements, and obedience to Him must come first. Many people are anointed by God, but so many exaggerate their position. If God only speaks to the head, then what use is the rest of the body? I need to be useful, but I have no desire to be in a leadership position. I will not be put in a position that would require me to go along with others or to adjust a message for fear of offending someone. The pastor and a prophet in unity would be a force to be reckoned with. I constantly pray, "Forgive me, Lord, for speaking when I shouldn't and for not speaking when I should. Help me to be obedient without hesitation, and to have a sound mind, the mind of Christ."

I am not the Holy Spirit for anyone, but I do know how important the Holy Spirit has been for me. The body of Christ has many parts, all of which are useful in building God's kingdom here on earth. There are many gifts, but there is only one God, and our thoughts are not His. Neither are our ways His ways. I am not impressed by famous people or megachurches, and I have no desire to promote the kingdom of humankind or any one person's fame.

I believe that my spirit is moved by God and that He stirs me to pray and to witness. His will must be done. The purpose for our salvation is to accomplish God's will, which requires us to be in in right relationship with Him. None are perfect, not even one, but God is drawn to a humble heart that is on fire. Moreover, He sees our intent.

PSYCHOLOGY

Pick up your mat, go home, and eat.
Your sins are forgiven, the shadow of Pete.

The Holy Spirit lives in you to sanctify,
To reveal what's true.

The past, the lack, lies, and abuse—
You've been bound by the devil's noose.
It's God's job to cut you loose.

Psychics and SOZO,
Theosophists and bozos,

They talk and ask questions; they shovel and pick;
They tell you they know what's making you tick.

The reality is, only one knows
What's in your heart and when to close
The wounds.

You come to the Lord just as you are.
He knows all your baggage;
He's brought you this far.

No pills, no frills, no couch, no clock,
No darkroom or candles, no incense or rocks.

If you could depend on unpleasant quirks,
On downers, on uppers, on mystical works,
You wouldn't have realized you needed a Savior
To rid you of your bad behavior.

So depend on the holy, the Spirit inside,
The gift that's given, to ready His bride.

He pours on the wine; it stings just a little.
He uses the oil, to heal and to settle.

He pays all debt and then carries you through.
He imparts His love, yes, even for you.

House Swept Clean

When a house is swept clean but is not maintained, it gets dirty all over again. Watchmen sit on the walls of the fellowship and watch for enemy activity. When given the signal from the Holy Spirit, they sound the alarm. Most times we want to keep the alarms set on silent so as not to frighten the sheep. In reality, we need to deal with the enemy so that the sheep will understand the effects of sin and its dangers. More importantly, we must practice discernment, which is the key to spiritual warfare and freedom. Without it you will be deceived.

Mercy is more powerful than judgment, and more effective; however, truth is what sets us free. Don't judge lest ye be judged. It is a hard thing to confront someone, especially someone in a position of leadership, with their blatant sin. You know yourself that you do not please God most days, and yet He asks you to shed light on someone else's sin. Get yourself cleaned up before the Lord and make sure He is sending you. Otherwise, you could cause an avalanche!

We have boundaries as Christians. If you don't know what they are, get your Bible out and start reading. I suggest starting in the New Testament. I started in the book of John and read through Revelation, and then I went back and started with Matthew and read through again. I also devoured the Proverbs for wisdom. I didn't dive into the Old Testament for a couple of years after my salvation, but when I did, the entire book made even more sense. I read Psalms, which I lovingly call the "crybaby book" because it makes me cry.

God loves us so much and wants to do for us far beyond what the world can offer, yet our minds and hearts are set on worldly things most of the time. I knew a pastor once who was trying to start a church. A small group of us attended the newly established church faithfully. People would come and go, checking us out, so we would have a few more at some services than at others. After each service, this pastor would get on

Facebook and go on about the awesome move of God. He would say that the crowd was large, that the altar was full, and that many had gotten saved. I wondered what service he went to after our service.

Exaggeration is a lie. We need only to be faithful to preach the Word so that God will add to us those who were being saved. The Holy Spirit does not need to be exaggerated. Unless you want the word *desolate* written over your sanctuary, you will not lie about God. The lying spirit comes in many forms with many faces. The liar is the deceiver, and his goal is to destroy before the Holy Spirit has a chance to work. God uses human beings, and so does the enemy. Something or someone may look good, smell good, feel good, or sound good, yet that person or thing may not be good. Do you think you have the discernment to know the difference? I have known saved, Spirit-filled champions of God who married scoundrels. The heart is made of flesh and can be deceived. So can the mind. But the well-oiled exercised spirit is hard to fool.

I was raised to accept and to seek spiritual things that were ungodly. I knew on the day I was saved how powerful God is and that what I had been following was weak and a lie. Being spiritual does not make you weird; you make it weird for yourself and for others by desiring attention. God desires obedience and He has perfect timing, yet we try to save people for Him, and we act spiritual out of arrogance and self-importance. Walking in the Spirit does not make you a powerful person; it makes you a powerful influence for God. If you are living in the Spirit, people will be drawn to you. You won't have to chase people down or bother them on a Saturday morning during your evangelical community outreach.

RELIGION

Religion varies in shape and size.
Doctrines twist;
Some are full of lies.

Interpretation involves desperation
To find a truth for your situation.

Inflation of sin to ruin a nation?
You become a sensation.

Lead the blind with a double mind.
The Word is subjective but never unkind.
Don't fall behind.

Bigger walls and wider halls,
Sanctuaries the size of malls.

What happens when the Spirit calls?
Can we let our programs fall?

Can we shut up shop at the coffee bar?
Stop buying and selling?
Did I go too far?

Is an hour or two enough for you?
Could you shred the program if He asked you to?

Who is the church?
Who runs the show?
Who plows the ground?
Who aims the bow?
Does anyone know?

Are your numbers adding up in a peculiar way?
Are people coming early and desiring to stay?
Does anyone show up to pray?

Do you look at the sheep and see dollar signs
Or warriors with renewed minds?

A man without vision shall perish.
So what's on the mind of the man?
Who's feeding him the plan?

I DARE YOU

What's your religion,
The hole in one?

Is it baseball,
Basketball,
Or shooting your gun?

How about the TV or the movie stars?
How about diamonds and shiny cars?

Is your favorite outing to the local bars?
What is it that sends you to Mars?

I dare you to ask,
"Is there more to this life?"
I dare you to knock
On His door for advice.

I dare you to seek
A look at His face.
I dare you to find

His amazing grace.

BE INNOCENT OF EVIL

Comparing religion is a waste of time. There are so many doctrines out there and so many beliefs, but there is only one Holy Spirit. Unity comes through the Holy Spirit of God, and where the Spirit of the Lord is, there is freedom. That is church.

I was not a churched person when I came to the Lord, so I had no doctrine or box of rules to follow. I didn't fear the Holy Spirit, because I had known the unholy spirits. Most of us have experience with the unholy but do not admit it. Every time you look at pornography or call the psychic hotline, you invite unholy spiritual activity into your home or your office and into your mind. Every time you get drunk, you are in danger of doing things or saying things you shouldn't because you are under the influence, or spell, of something unholy. I wonder how many parents give no thought to buying their kids an Ouija board or a Magic 8-Ball?

It is disturbing to me that Christians are comfortable with horror movies and after-school TV shows with themes of divination, necromancy, witchcraft, wizardry, magic, and other nonsense the Bible warns us to stay away from. We are called to be innocent of evil.

Christians fear the spiritual yet commune with it and put out the welcome mat for it every day. The spiritual life is either good or evil. The Bible tells us that in the last days people will be lovers of themselves and will accept false doctrines. The Bible is talking to the church and about the church. The world is already deceived; however, I have met many unsaved people who have more discernment than many of the Christians I know.

MAGIC

What is magic?
Is there any real power?

Pull the rabbit out of the hat.
Surprise me with a flower,

Or build me a tower.

Hocus-pocus hullabaloo,
A wave of my wand to put a curse on you.

How about a tail or two?

It is amazing what people will do,
Always searching but never finding

What's really true.

COMPETITION

Church has become a competitive sport. I watch as one builds a bigger gymnasium or another builds a skate park or youth center. Instead of ministering to the unsaved, we cater to them as if having the coolest stuff is going to bring deliverance to a broken, abused, or neglected heart. All works of the flesh are dead unless they are driven by the Holy Spirit and the motives are pure.

I spent three years ministering to college- and career-age adults. They were drawn by the truth, structure, discipline, and food. Young people desire clean lines in the sand and wish to know that someone cares enough to tell them the truth and to spend time with them. They need to know that they are valuable. In college they are one in a thousand or so, and after college they are trying to stick out among the crowded workforce. They need stability and a place of safety where they can find encouragement to stand when it is not popular to do so.

It is baffling to me that there are so many different denominations, doctrines, and interpretations of the Bible, so I can understand how, with everything else that is on the mind of a student or young parent, confusing it must be to find a church family—maybe to the point of giving up.

Young people are looking for something real. There are so many trends and gimmicks, but shouldn't it be the Holy Spirit who draws the crowd? When the church was first being built, the Word was preached and God was adding to their numbers daily people who were being saved. The early church did not have the latest sound system or a theatrical atmosphere, and I am sure that most of their instruments were very crude, yet they led worship and the people responded. People were saved, healed, and delivered of demonic strongholds, and became part of the church. Those who were afraid or offended, or very deeply indoctrinated, did not.

I believe that God uses the culture around us to draw people to Him, but you can never replace the Word, the truth, or worship with the world. Our ways are not His ways, and our thoughts are not His thoughts. And if we are not careful, all our plans will come to nothing.

A man without vision shall perish because he can't see. He can't see beyond his own thoughts because Jesus is the one who opens a person's eyes to God's plan. The plans of human beings are many, but they mostly come to nothing.

MANY ROADS

We focus on statistics;
We focus on the trends.

We want a "hook" to win the lost.
The banter never ends.

Start something new.
Use a new cru.

Simply use some newer words so everyone will follow you
Into the ditch.

So easy to make the switch.

What once was wrong now is right.
Tolerance,
An open mind;
There is no need to fight.

All roads
Are the same.
All gods have the same name.

This life is just a game.

No need to choose.
You can never, ever lose.

God is love,
So hit the snooze.

WHO'S AFRAID?

Who's afraid of the big bad wolf?

No one.

Entertainment,
Telephones,
TV, and megaloans.

Breathe life into the dry bones.

We give away the gifts we're given
As if we bought them cheap.

The righteous life is life worth living;
The rest is but a heap
To burn.

Learn to bless.
Scrap the mess.
There's so much more to learn.

This life is but a single test.
The next is what you earn.

Phony Baloney

Just a phony baloney,
Nothing real to see.

A wink to think there's an inside joke,
But a joke is what you'll be.

The Bible is the key.
The truth will set you free.

You offer nothing to the sheep.
You've put them all to sleep.

Remember that the seeds you sow
Will be the ones you reap.

Hot or Cold?

Unfortunately, a church will have a surge of popularity, only to become anemic again. Church leaders go round and round the mountain, wondering what the next hook should be. Are we winning the lost or just filling the seats and paying the bills? When sheep are not being fed, they tend to scatter eventually.

I have visited churches of several denominations, as well as many nondenominational fellowships, over the years. What they all have in common is worship, the reading of the bulletin, and the preaching of the Word. I have heard the parable of the Good Samaritan taught with a couple of different interpretations; I have heard the "hot or cold" sermon taught with very lukewarm understanding of the Holy Spirit; and I have watched in horror as those who go to the altar are nudged to fall down. I have been slain in the spirit only three times in twenty years and no one was touching me. I can tell you exactly what God removed from me and what He imparted to me. Faking a spiritual move does nothing for you. It also aggrieves God. It is a lie and people are watching. Many unsaved people have pretty sharp discernment!

I prayed for God to change me and to deliver me from behaviors that were not honoring to Him. Each time I was slain, I had been praying over the course of several months for a specific change, because no matter how hard I'd tried to overcome, I failed. So the first time I was slain, I was visiting a church in Lincoln, Illinois, and I went to the altar for prayer. Up to this point, any time someone tried to nudge me, I would resist because I was not being moved by God. I was standing there when the prophet was making his way toward me, but he had stopped two people down from me to pray. I could not hear him speak except to say, *"Holy Spirit and fire!"* I was out and down before I knew what hit me. He was not in front of me and he was not touching me. He was not even praying for me!

While I was down, I could see two angels holding a black pot over me full of hot coals. I felt fear for a moment, but then I felt kindness and peace. They poured the hot coals into the center of my chest, which seemed to be laid open. I could feel the coals burning, but they were not burning me. I sat up and started to feel sick, so I opened my eyes. I was fighting against my own healing. Suddenly aware of where I was, I had to crawl to my seat. As I sat down, I leaned back, exhausted, but I was totally sober and very aware of my surroundings. No one was paying attention to me, thank goodness!

When I awoke the next morning, I turned to my husband and told him that I loved him. This was something we never said to each other. I had been asking God to set me free to love and to trust love. He did.

God's love is truth, and it's the truth that sets us free, no matter how it makes us feel or how offended we are in the moment. Truth is love. Covering over a multitude of sins does not mean to ignore sin; it means to cover that person in love and mercy while helping them to find relief. God is mercy, and He is the only one who can extend mercy through us. You don't have the power to pardon someone's sin; no person does. We simply lead others to the water, and then God deals with the heart.

A true friend will risk your friendship for the sake of your soul. Repeating a problem over and over is not healing; it is regurgitating. Healing comes through repentance and forgiveness, and repentance comes through the truth. Avoiding the truth is cowardice, whereas speaking the truth takes courage.

The reason many Christians are so depressed and so focused on their problems is because they don't know the Savior. Instead of focusing on yourself every day, why not try beginning the day by being thankful to God and practicing entering His rest? Our society is sick, and so is God's church. Being I or me focused will not do anyone any good.

Are you special?

A re you born again? Are you obedient, forgiving, loving, patient, kind, truthful, honest, fearless, prayerful, discerning?

The unrepentant, unsaved soul believes that feelings should be given much attention. I am sorry, but the problem with many Christians is that they have too many feelings and not enough *faith*! They treat God like a vending machine. People need an excuse to continue sinning, so they blame God for their disappointments and losses. Those who barely know God see their glass as half empty instead of half full, and see loss as punishment instead of protection.

Christians are not to be led by their eyes, ears, or feelings but by the Holy Spirit. I may have a Bible study group and inevitably there will be one person who comes every week desperate for prayer for the same things they needed prayer for ten years ago. This person demands lots of attention and holds the study group hostage with story after poor-pitiful-me story, never having a victorious testimony.

We all have concerns and illnesses and stresses in this life, but we are to focus on the life after this one. When we come to the Lord, we make a commitment to Him to serve Him and to be the best example of who He is through us. In order for Him to work through us, we have to allow Him to change us. Paul acknowledged that he didn't know how to pray as he ought. Peter denied Jesus three times. Thomas didn't recognize resurrected Jesus and asked for proof that the resurrected Lord was who He said He was. We all fall short of the glory of God and we are all a work in progress until the day we die, but the goal is to serve the Lord.

Prayer is conversation with the Lord, whether on your knees or driving your car. Instead of giving the Lord your laundry list every time you pray, try adoring Him. Try to focus on Him and not on yourself. Tell Him how much you love Him and trust Him with your life. Pray for His will to be done, not yours.

Before salvation, it's all about us and our feelings, hopes, and dreams. When we are born again, God replaces our feelings with His healings, and our hopes and dreams with His plans and schemes. He created us for fellowship and to build His church, but all we want is to build is our own ministry, bank account, and reputation.

Ask yourself how you would have reacted to being thrown in jail for talking about Jesus and then having your feet shackled to the floor. Really, think about it. You are shackled to the floor, so how do you go to the bathroom? You are there next to your friend and probably around other prisoners with the guards looking on. You are expected to relieve yourself in your pants where you sit. I don't know if Jesus's disciples were given food or water when they were imprisoned.

So what did they do in this awful situation? They sang songs to the Lord, praising and worshipping. They rejoiced in their situation—*despite* their situation! They were not concerned about their own pain and discomfort. When the apostles were told by the authority not to preach Jesus, they chose to obey God instead—and wound up in prison.

In their position, I can see myself crying and asking, "Why me, God? Why would You do this to me?" Some people might go crazy or try to commit suicide, and some would curse God and pray to die.

I knew a woman who passed from cancer. She'd known she had cancer for several years before going home to be with the Lord. The day I met her, she told me that as soon as the Lord healed her, she would lay hands on the sick and they would be healed. I looked at her puzzled and asked her why she was waiting. I tried to encourage her to get on about the business of God now, today, because it was her commission to lay hands on the sick and to proclaim them healed. Sadly, she felt that she needed to be healed first. She died within a month or so of that meeting.

We are told to obey authority, but we are not to compromise our faith, ignore truth, lie, or disobey God. We are never called to please human beings over God or to put our feelings, problems, or comfort ahead of the will of God. Repenting and giving your life to Christ is a choice, and we will all give account for our actions before Jesus.

Some Christians will cast out demons and heal the sick, but they may be doing these things for the praise of human beings or for money and fame. There will be many people of lawlessness who come performing signs miracles and wonders. Will you have the discernment it takes to know the good from the bad, the truth from a lie? When we come before Jesus, He will know the heart and mind of every person and will know the motives of all. "Depart from me; I never knew you" scares me more than anything. This life is not about me. It is all about Him.

Superspiritual people talk about generational curses and assignments against people as if these things were just a flea you could flick off your shoulder. They pair up every ailment with a sin. My sins have been forgiven and I belong to the Lord, so if I am sinning against Him, I will be convicted and I will repent. We were never promised a life free from problems and disappointments. There are Christians who talk a lot about things they really know nothing about. I have been around spiritual people, and I know that the truly spiritual don't talk as much as they pray. The truly spiritual are not looking to get attention or sympathy; they are busy giving their attention to God. They are watching and listening.

I have been around pastors who are quick to make excuses, quick to discount a prophet, quick to cover over a rumor, quick to hide the truth, quick to forgive but slow to correct, and quick to show mercy but slow to repent, ignoring God's timing. Love covers over a multitude of sins, but it never hides them.

WHICH WAY DO WE GO?

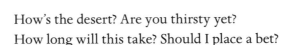

How's the desert? Are you thirsty yet?
How long will this take? Should I place a bet?

How's that mountain? Can you see from the top?
The pain from your effort, will it ever stop?

You plan and you plan, appoint and anoint,
Ask for more money. Isn't that the point?

All so busy, busy, but who's being changed?
Serve till you're dizzy; get those chairs rearranged

Oh what a mess. We reap what we sow,
Doing our best with what we know.

My question is, "Who has the plan?"
Who has the plan to influence man?

His thoughts are not ours,
So how do we know?
His ways are not ours,

So which way do we go?

WHAT ARE YOU WAITING FOR?

What are you waiting for?
Do you need me to show you the door?

You have to open it.

I can lead you to water,
But you gotta drink.

I can tell you a thing,
But you gotta think.

I can open the Word and share the reward,
But you get bored.

Your mind is on the things you horde.

I can turn on the worship;
Will you hear the truth?

Conviction doesn't feed your sweet tooth.

Let me know when you need Him;
I'll be glad to show you the way.

The Holy Spirit is waiting;
Salvation is free today.

This is between the two of you,
Not about you and me.

Jesus takes the blinders off.
The question is, do you want to see?

I AM A WORK IN PROGRESS

W hen the Holy Spirit isn't in the lead, humankind is. I have had leaders tell me that because they were positioned by God and anointed by Him, everything they do is from God. The congregation is not to question anything the leadership decides, even if it is to interpret the scripture differently or to teach in a way that is more seeker-friendly than Spirit-friendly.

The Bible tells us that the whole church is valuable and usable to God. God also appoints and anoints people to a certain fellowship to watch over the house. If the pastor has all the answers, why would God need prophets or watchmen?

Being assigned to a leadership position comes with more responsibility and accountability than others in the church have. Elders are to help the pastor, but they are also there to keep the leaders in check. The elders are an accountability team, serving as protection for the church. Many leaders ignore the elders and do their own thing. This kind of thinking is arrogant and out of sync with the Word.

A prophet has to swallow a lot of criticism and accusation. It is more important to obey God than to worry about the opinion or reaction of human beings. It doesn't matter what you are struggling with personally. The enemy is the accuser. The delivery of a prophetic message or warning is done in obedience to God, not humankind. The message is for the benefit of humankind, from God. The accuser will do all that he can to keep you quiet, even accusing you or illuminating your every flaw, to discount you as a prophet.

I must make it clear, though, that even with this being the case, God cannot and will not use a liar—and lying includes exaggeration—to deliver His Word. Prophetic people can deliver muddy, controlling, or pleasing messages for their own gain. This does nothing but put a stain on the prophetic ministry. God desires all to live righteously though none are perfect, not even one. His standards for me have been made clear: use no alcohol or other depressants or stimulants, have no addictions, use clean language, listen to God-honoring music, watch no R-rated movies, engage in no idolatry, have humility, have love for the church, continue in Bible study, practice obedience, engage in fasting, and keep praying. I am a work in progress.

CAN YOU SEE?

God giveth and taketh. He made the land,
Formed humankind with His very own hand.

The trees He made for rest and breeze,
For fire and fuel so man wouldn't freeze.

A home for bees. Honey.
Tap for sap and then take a nap.

Mighty oak, branches wide, like the wings of God, to hide inside.
A nesting place as the sun hits your face.

Ride the wind that blows through the tree
On a swing provided to cradle thee.

Can you see?
He's always watching you and me.

POLITICALLY CORRECT

I am not concerned with being politically correct, and at times I seem impolite. Nevertheless, I do try to be honest. In most services I want to scream and shout that Jesus is alive. We sing to the ceiling, our minds consumed by debt and bills, lies and desires. We preach to please our audience or to guilt them into giving more money. God does not need our money, but He does need obedience from us and for our hearts to be charitable. He is much more concerned about your heart than about your wallet. If the church had a right heart toward giving, then the preacher could preach on another subject. So I would throw this question on to the pastor: Why doesn't your church have a right and fundamental attitude toward tithing?

When I was a child and a preacher from town would come to visit, Mother would cuss and scream that all he wanted was money. Even as a child I would wonder why these preachers would bother with us then. The poor pastors who visited us got an earful from Mother. I thank God today for every one of them, and I ask God to bless them in abundance.

I am constantly being told that no church is perfect, that churches are made up of people who are flawed just like me. But there is an attitude that you are in rebellion if you are not in unity with the leadership. If you are not in unity, then you must have a Jezebel spirit and a spirit of gossip. You are told that prayer meetings are just a breeding ground for gossip, or that one doesn't run out on one's "family" over a disagreement. "We are afraid that if you pray in tongues, it will scare people." I have heard it all—excuses for ignoring God and His power.

If congregants are afraid of the Holy Spirit and of speaking in tongues, maybe the church leaders should teach them about the Holy Spirit. Maybe they should talk about the demonic garbage coming from congregants' TVs and radios that doesn't seem to scare them in the least.

I do not understand the preacher who uses the pulpit to expel his aggravation. This action is immature and prideful. If a family gets up and leaves at a certain time, it could simply mean that they have a standing plan on Sunday. It could mean that someone is diabetic and they need to eat. It could mean a lot of things. A couple may even complain that a service goes on too long and they have to leave because their kids are no longer paying attention and becoming agitated. I can understand. If you feel the need to preach or hold the congregants for three or four hours, just do it. Don't get up there and immaturely start laughing or making jokes about people who don't like to stay over the lunch hour. Or worse, don't allege they don't want as much of God as the rest of the crowd, which evidently gives you license to insult them and accuse them of something that may not be true. No matter the situation, the pulpit should never be used by the pastor in such a manner. It is arrogant, prideful, sickening, immature, and ugly. This does not honor God in any way.

It is okay to disagree with the leadership. It does not make you rebellious, or a jezebel, or even a gossip. If you are those things, then repent and seek deliverance. I have heard pastors and other leaders say, "Don't touch God's anointed." Well, I am God's anointed too, so maybe they should be careful about the names they call me and about the things they accuse me of doing.

Why does God use prophets? Why did God appoint elders? God has put an accountability process in place because He knows that we all have visions of grandeur and we all desire the worship and praise. This is not new. Lucifer, the most beautiful angel, fell from grace because he desired the worship and adoration being given to God. He did not leave alone. In rebellion, he took one-third of the angelic population with him. Eve wanted to be like God, and her actions put her out of paradise. The enemy knew just how to tempt Eve. He accused God of being a liar and a deceiver, of withholding something valuable from them. The serpent told Eve that God did not want her to be like Him and assured her that if she ate the fruit, she would not die but, indeed, would be like God. "Who told you that you would die?" He knew exactly who told her, and why.

Then Adam approached. And though He walked and talked with God daily, he believed Eve, because there she stood … alive. She had eaten the fruit and had not died. So instead of obeying the very one who had given him rule and reign, the one who provided so lavishly for him and

Eve, the one He had intimate fellowship with, Adam believed Eve, the woman, and the serpent. He took a bite. The moment he bit, their eyes were opened to their nakedness. Shame and guilt were born. Not until Adam had taken a bite did their eyes open. He had been given rule and reign, and the woman was the helpmate (his helper and support). The man gave his authority over to the woman, who gave it to the enemy. They were removed from the garden. When confronted by God, Adam blamed the woman.

God withholds things from us for our own good. Try thinking on that the next time you feel slighted by God. Maybe what you desire isn't what you need.

The only way of escape is through the blood of Jesus. When you meet Jesus, you can blame all the people who influenced you, but Jesus will hold only you accountable for your relationship, or lack thereof, with Him. You make choices every day whether to follow humankind or to know the Lord.

THAT'S WHAT THEY SAY

Keep your friends close;
Keep your enemies closer.

That's what they say.
Yeah, that's what they say.

Women bite and devour each other.

That's what they say,
Yeah, that's what they say.

Men compete to one-up one another,
Not considering each other a brother.

That's what they say,
Yeah, that's what they say.

Which is the way?

Should I turn to the right?
Should I go left to avoid a fight?
The middle keeps me up all night.

Christians say that God is the light,
But then they live in the gray till they lose their sight—
No line in the sand, no black or white.

That's what they say.

Anyway,

That's what they say.

We need to give God our every day,
Be true to the Spirit,

Despite what they say.

PROGRESS

A t fifty-seven, I've lived through lots of fashion change, only to wind up wearing the same styles I wore forty years ago. My daughters respond to me the same way I responded to my mother when she told me, "We wore those when I was in junior high." I lived through the sixties, through the Kennedy assassination and a walk on the moon; through the seventies, including disco; through the eighties, when I was married, had children, and did Jazzercise; and through the nineties, which I spent drunk and seeking psychics to find out when or if I was ever going to be happy.

So here we are in 2017. I'm typing on a laptop, reading the news, and checking the weather, which, by the way, I can do on my iPhone. The huge cellular phones came out in the 1990s, and I had one. You couldn't carry it in your purse, but you were really cool if you had one in your car. Those phones screamed success!

I grew up in the day when we had a party line and all the neighbors could listen to your conversations. I also lived in a house with no indoor plumbing. The outhouse was a few feet from the back door. I learned to get over my fear of spiders using that outhouse, because it was always filled with daddy-long-legs!

It's amazing how things change. Today Yahoo! news goes from Kim Kardashian, to the Clintons' many scandals, to the latest terror attack by radicals. The national debt alone (in the trillions) is reason to be in a state of panic. I am not at all surprised about the condition of the United States and of the world overall. I am not surprised because I know what the Word of God says about these things. Any Christian who studies the Bible should not be surprised about what is going on around us.

The worldwide church is what puzzles me. Reiki, yoga, and even magic has been accepted inside the doors of many fellowships, as well as into the homes of many Christians. Practitioners serve as deacons, elders, and Sunday school teachers, and they lead our youth. People are not taking the time to discover the truth about yoga; they just like how it makes them feel. To the Hindu and the Buddhist, I am sure that it is awesome to have God's church spending time, money, and influence paying homage to their gods, as opposed to worshipping the God of heaven.

Do you assume that because someone is becoming a member of your organization, they are saved and ready to serve? Are you spending time with the flock at all, or are you busy with community affairs and meetings? It is not the job of any pastor to be a politician.

What good is a leadership meeting if you can't lead your own sheep?

The Word is our spiritual nourishment. It soothes our soul, erases doubt, worry, and fear, imparts wisdom and knowledge, and reveals all truth. The Word of God sets the captive free and heals the sick. The Word sweeps the house clean, leaving little to no room for the enemy. Try meditating on the Word to get your day started.

YOGA

Yoga, toga, pudding and pie.
Worship in pose until you cry.

None the wiser; all free today.
Spirit guide is on his way.

Release control and into the hole you go.

An open door is a welcome sign
To anything that wants to find
A way into your mind.

Off with her head; wish you were dead.
To rabbits for tea and philosophy.

Delusion is from the enemy.

Take up your sword, sharpen the blade,
Mince the mess the soul has made.

An empty mind is led astray.

No black or white—just shades of gray.

Giving is an Act of Obedience

———◆———

Too many Christians have visions of grandeur. I believe more ministry happens in small groups or other intimate settings. If you have a right heart toward the church, your fellowship will grow and prosper spiritually and physically. If you try to manipulate and control, or if you continue to ignore the Holy Spirit, your plans will come to nothing and there will be gossip and slander and dissension. There will be repeated splits, sin will abound, and eventually you will experience desolation.

We admire these larger-than-life ministries and even covet them. Many sheep do not know their pastors, having never even met them. Many of them are following an "ideal" and never experience a move of the Spirit. Your pastor cannot be your God, but he should be a source of spiritual maturity. In the end it is up to you to pick up your Bible and read. It is up to you to surrender your life to Christ and to become dependent on Him. It is up to you to develop a relationship with God (Holy Spirit) and to become a strong conduit for the sake of others.

Pastors and leaders have a responsibility toward you, but you are responsible for picking up your mantle and filling your own lamp. The pastor's job is to encourage you to look up and not out, to ask, seek, and knock, and to be honest in every single thing going on in the church. There is no room for deception, lying, lack of discernment, or cover-up in the head. God will reveal the truth if we do not.

I had a pastor who told me that his sheep should reflect or mimic him, but the reality is that the sheep should reflect Jesus. If the pastor is living a spiritual, obedient life, he will encourage His flock to gain knowledge of Jesus and also to live a spiritual, righteous, and obedient life.

I would like to encourage pastors and leaders to come to know the spiritual temperature of their church. God has given you an army, a body full of gifts. If you ignore those whom God has planted among you, you will certainly miss out. Not all the sheep are spiritually mature, but it is your job to shepherd them. It is your job to lead the sheep to Jesus and help them to realize all that God has for them. The sheep are God's army. If you are not training them, correcting them, and encouraging them, then you are not doing your job. Know your sheep, and know that they have been fostered to you for a time. And time is getting short. Do not frustrate those who are spiritual. Even if they make you uncomfortable, they belong to God.

God assigns watchmen to every fellowship. Watchmen are used to protect the flock and to sound the alarm at any sign of enemy activity. Watchmen pray while you are sleeping, travail while you are dreaming, and conduct spiritual warfare while you are resting. Some of them may seem weird to you, but they have their place. Indeed, there is a place for all who are obedient.

I do not attend church to pay the rent or to serve simply wherever there is an open slot. I belong to the body of Christ to bring forth God's will. I have never had a problem with tithing. Indeed, I am a cheerful giver. A mature fellowship will be well supported and content in every season. Tithing should be the natural response of a joyful heart. Salvation is free, so we do not owe God anything—and we cannot buy His favor. However, it is our job to support the church and pay the bills. If you want a financially healthy church, feed the sheep a healthy, spiritually nourishing meal.

Giving is an act of obedience, and it comes with a promise, but never forget that Jesus paid all of our debt and you cannot buy God's love.

No Voice

Suffer in silence,
Losing sleep.

Don't tell, don't tell;
Don't you make a peep.

Little girls and little boys
Should listen to their masters.

Sister Sue and Brother Bill
Should listen to their pastors.

Is anybody watching the masters and the pastors?

God is.

Your stock is but a heap,
Rewards you didn't earn.

What you sow is what you'll reap.
Don't you ever learn?

I'm warning you to feed my sheep,
Or your barn is going to burn!

It's All Good

Community.
Serve to serve.
God grades on a curve.

Welcome all;
Rebuke none:
Russian roulette without the gun.

The New Church

When someone complains that ministry is stressful and wearing them out, I want to tell them that it's time for a break. For some, complaining about being overworked gives them a sense of self-importance. Some are afraid that no one else could do what they do, or do it the way they would. Some are afraid they won't get the credit if they don't do it all themselves.

What if someone messes up? I can tell you for sure that the world will not come to an end and that most all things can be corrected.

I do not believe that it is God's will for you to be stressed in ministry. I am not saying there won't be stress. After all, you will be working with people. Teaching the Word and praying with others should be an encouragement. Maybe we lean on our own understanding and talents more than we lean on God. He is our relief, our provision, our strength, our wisdom, our knowledge, and our courage. We all need God's direction and correction, but mostly we need humility and faith.

Are you asking Him for direction, or are you planning for next year using your own thoughts and desires? Too many churches are run like well-oiled machines and leave no room for healing, deliverance, salvation, or even joy. We want what we want, and we want it now. Humankind is on the throne. It's an all-good, all-inclusive, peacekeeping love fest—the new church.

LEADER

If you're overworked, overtired,
Overstressed, and overadmired,
You're in the wrong position.

Submission—
You gotta know the drill.

Timing's key and nothing's free.
God pays the bill.

Delegation is a skill.
It gets you over that hill

Without killing you.

He will give the order.
Simply bend your ear.
His will is what He whispers

Does anybody hear?

COEXIST

God's fire, which comes through His Holy Spirit, comes to consume, to separate, and to purify. In the presence of God, can a person stand? In the presence of God, there is no need for preaching or singing, because in His presence truth is revealed. Who, in God's presence, would not be repentant?

The Word tells us that God came not to bring peace, but war. So if Jesus is the Prince of Peace, what is God trying to tell us by saying this? The war is between our flesh and the spirit, and there can only be one winner. In the world, there will always be wars and rumors of war, because humankind has the need to control, to seize, to own, and to manipulate.

I am sure you have seen the "Coexist" stickers, as if the answer to peace is to agree with and accept anything. The Christian is to discern between what is good and acceptable to God and what is not, and to turn from the latter. Religion or lack thereof cannot determine which laws you conform to. In order to coexist, all must adhere to a set of standards and laws that protect all for the good and well-being of all. We have to coexist because there are millions of humans who live on this planet; however, not everything is good for us.

If a pedophile desires to have sex with children and claims that he was born with this drive, does that make it okay for him to molest children? Of course not. Are we not to resist evil or evil desires opposed by God? If a person is a kleptomaniac, is that a disease they were born with? Should it be okay for them to steal because they claim to have been born that way? Of course not. It is not okay to murder someone. If two men or two women desire a sexual relationship, it is their right to engage in one; it is between the two of them. I know what God's Word says about it, though, so I cannot agree that it is a good or natural thing, but I would never treat such people in any other way than with respect and kindness. I coexist with all kinds of people every day and I do not agree with them on many things; however, I will not agree with a person or rebuke God's Word for the sake of that individual's feelings.

I love Jesus and I want to serve Him. I am sure people who know me have their opinions about that. The lost seek only to satisfy the desires of the flesh. A Christian lives to please the Lord.

> So I say, walk by the Spirit, and you will not gratify the desires of the flesh. For the flesh desires what is contrary to the Spirit, and the Spirit what is contrary to the sinful nature. They are in conflict with each other, so that you do not do whatever you want. But if you are led by the Spirit, you are not under law. (Galatians 5:16)

> Those who belong to Christ Jesus have crucified the flesh with its passions and desires. Since we live by the Spirit, let us keep in step with the Spirit. Let us not become conceited, provoking and envying each other. (Galatians 5:24)

> Brothers and sisters, if someone is caught in a sin, you who live by the Spirit should restore that person gently. But watch yourselves, or you also may be tempted. (Galatians 6:1)

A NARROW GATE

A narrow gate,
The great escape.
Thread the needle.
Cash is bait.

A camel through.
I relate.
To catch a thief;
Love can wait.

Money in and money out.
The liar's hire, there's no doubt.

Clout without honor.

The love of money will surely kill.
Keep living for a fleshly thrill.

Someone has to pay the bill.

So why the wasted worship?
Money can't buy love.

The gate is narrow the road is wide.
Keep running
Till there's no place left to hide.

THE FOOL

A foolish man
Builds his house upon the sand,

Plants his seed among the thorns,

Hits the bar then drives his car,
Pulls the bull by its horns.

He never heeds the caution sign.

Monkey see, monkey do,
But whom does monkey answer to?

Adultery

To dishonor your spouse,
To embarrass your house,

Makes you a louse.

GREED

The seed
That's carried away.
The need for more consumes each day.
Is your house made of straw or hay?
It could be blown away.

Then all the things
Of your hopes and dreams

Become rubble.

The storms of life
In season bring strife.
You want without delay.

Can you see the decay?

A new car is old before it leaves the lot.
Your shoes are hurting you—the ones you just bought.
Gold is the future, or maybe not.
The food in the fridge is beginning to rot.

To have or to have not.

Is that really the question?

VANITY

Vanity is a worthless word;
Arrogance,
Even more absurd.

Look in the mirror. What do you see?
A selfish shell who isn't free.

You love the sound of your own voice.
Assume that you will be the choice.

Fame.
The attention is all you seek,
While you overlook the spiritually weak.

With self on the mind, it's hard to find
Time,

Time for the Word,
To visit the Lord.
Praying and waiting,
You get so bored.

It's lonely up there on top of your hill.
What's now a burden was once a thrill.

To honor the Lord was your desire.

Without the Spirit,
You're just noise for hire.

ENVY

Rotting bones fill the thrones.

Flattery like sugar cones.

Seek the things your neighbor owns.

He has what you want.
You want what you see.
If you can't have it, why should he?

Envy.

LITTLE WHITE LIE

Time flies. Go on with your life.
Go through the motions,
Avoiding strife.

Ignore the truth as days go by.
Live in a vacuum and never cry.

Why?

What's wrong with a little white lie?
It's not like I'm going to die.

Am I?

So I fudge a little; what's the big deal?
Whom does it hurt?
It's not like it's real.

It's not as if I'm trying to steal!

CONVICTION

Nothing helps. I'm in too deep.
I pray the Lord my soul to keep.

I know I'm saved—I love the Lord—
So how do I cut this umbilical cord?

Conviction, repentance, repeat.
Conviction, repentance, repeat.

Interrupted sleep; I'm counting sheep.

I'm running away all over again.
God's patience must be wearing thin.

This barking dog that's chasing me
Says that he's my friend.

In my dream he holds the key
To freedom.

Will this cycle ever end?

FOR THE SAKE OF OTHERS

W hen people come to me with issues, they at times act as if God is holding out on them. After I listen to them, I ask how long they have been holding out on God. I want to know if they blame God for all their personal failures and tragedies, but I also want to remind them that this is not a one-sided relationship. Are you actively pursuing God? Are you living a more righteous life today than you were on the day you got saved?

God can do anything and He knows all things, but He will not give you the desires of your heart if those desires are not good for you. He wants to give us new desires as we are being sanctified, transformed. When we come to the Lord, we come in a surrendered position, giving all to God and allowing the Holy Spirit to give us eyes to see, ears to hear, a sound mind to know the mind of Christ, and a heart at peace.

In the surrendered position we give up our right to be right and we exchange our will for obedience.

We live in a society where depravity is celebrated and righteousness is despised.

Our nation's problems didn't start with adultery, idolatry, debt, lying, drug addiction, divorce, and so forth. Our nation's issues stem from the pledges and the unholy, unrighteous covenants we have made. Our condition is revealed by the symptoms we display. Pride and arrogance are what drove Lucifer from heaven, Adam and Eve from the garden, and kings from their thrones, and these things are the driving force behind many a pastor who winds up losing his pulpit or position. Our elected leaders at all levels and from all facets of society, including the church, sneak around, lie, flatter, and deceive, all while plumping up their bank accounts, taking bribes, and making unholy alliances.

The things that I write are motivated by the things God has been showing me over the last twenty years. For example, I have observed that money is a powerful force that can trap and influence a church, causing the affected church to reflect the government.

In the political arena, we have people vying for civil service jobs paid by the people, ostensibly to work for the people. I believe that most politicians tell us what we want to hear in order to get elected. Most know they won't accomplish much of what they promise. However, those individuals who are feeding their political machine will have their favors taken care of first—at the cost of the people.

We are told to open our hearts, close our mouths, give money, and share, share, share. The church and the government can easily be compared today. One is a reflection of the other, humankind building a kingdom for humankind. The leaders are in on the secrets and lies, and the sheep are simply grazing. We must pray for accountability and integrity in our leaders. The Holy Spirit can bring conviction if we will only pray.

The whole body is called to pray regardless if one is a brand-new Christian or a seasoned one. When we pray together, we are encouraging one another and teaching each other. Like stone on stone, we smooth each other out. The grazing sheep will wake up one day and realize that they have been had. I tell you now that your pastor will not be with you on the day you come face-to-face with Jesus. It will be you and Jesus, and you will be the only one giving an account of your life. This relationship is between you and God alone.

Nothing is free, and the only voice we are called to follow is the voice of the Lord. Now your pastor or leaders may be anointed and even obedient, but it is up to you to discern. You are responsible for positioning yourself under right leadership. Also, you should be growing spiritually wherever you are. You should be changing and becoming able to share all that you have experienced through your new relationship. We should all have testimonies piled up, just waiting for God to use them for someone's sake.

SOS

Consumed with outer space,
Neglecting this Peyton Place,

Living greener just in case
The icebergs are all erased.

God's church is in disgrace.

Global warming, the IRS,
Fear to rear *distress*.

Is this a test?

I'm sending God an SOS.

WARNING SIGNS

Backward,
Forward,
Inside out:
This nation's doing a face-about.

Right is wrong and wrong is right.
Few put up a fight.

Seduction,
Hypnotic change, and blame.
Leaders seeking fame.

With stars in our eyes we give the prize
To the one who tells the biggest lies.

Depravity.
All is free.
Make believe a money tree.

The changes that I see
Were prophesied through history.

I beg of you to read the Word.
It's proof of all you've heard,

Warning signs by God's design,

Urging us to toe the line.

PIED PIPER

All free today!

Pied Piper leads the way

Into the ditch. There's always a hitch.
Someone has to pay.

Hi-ho, hi-ho,
I'm off to work, but wouldn't you know,
My boss has let me go.
He couldn't afford to pay my wage—
Hired someone half my age.

With all the lies they tell and all the polls they take,
It's hard to gauge the jobless rate.

Life should never be up for debate.

Factions and friction,
Regulatory restriction.

Pay the tax,
Tax the pay,
Tax the tax,
And call it a day.

Is this the road that leads the way?

THAT STILL SMALL VOICE

There are politicians who call themselves Christians but who, without a prompter, do not know scripture. It is embarrassing to listen to them stumble over the Word of God. There are those who talk like Christians and quote scripture all the time, but they are merely clanging cymbals. Like many church members, they are acting.

There are righteous men and women who want to do the right thing, but how will you know these from the others? As a Christian, how do you know who is talking trash and who is striving for righteousness? Discernment is a gift from the Holy Spirit. Some people call it intuition. I believe we all do have some knowing in our spirits, because the Holy Spirit is always trying to get our attention and trying to protect us. God knows beyond what we can see or hear. We are called to be a spiritual people, but most of us have a hard time getting over our flesh.

The intuition or knowing, that gut feeling, is the Holy Spirit communicating to your spirit to warn you, to guide you, and to help you. The Holy Spirit is testing us and training us to pay attention to that still small voice and to obey it. I can be in a store with my grocery or supply list, but something will cross my mind or I will see an item and wonder if I need it. I will choose to pass by it because it is not on the list, only to get home and find that I am out of the item. You may think this is a small thing and that God does not have time for such nonsense, but if so you are wrong.

God gives us all that we need to live righteous lives. I did not say perfect or self-righteous lives, but righteous lives. Being righteous is of the heart, not just action of the flesh. God knows our hearts, and He knows which of us desire to serve him and to walk in truth. You cannot fool Him. He knows what you are hiding and why you are hiding it. If you desire righteousness, then *surrender!* It is that simple.

ADDICTION

An addiction is not a disease.
You can't fix it with a pill or a drill.

You start the fight,
Give it flight,
Add more to increase the thrill.

And you want me to pay the bill?

Use it to lose it.
Use it to excuse it.

Your crutch, not mine.

No one makes you play the game,
But you'll have to pay the fine.

The hold is strong.

You play with the noose to get it loose,
Flirting with the line.

There's no excuse for this abuse.

Be careful;
You may run out of time.

GIVE ME A PILL

Feelin' blue,
Confused.

Give me a pill.

Responsibility ain't thrillin' me.

Give me a pill.

Work for what?
Work for whom?
Paying taxes is all I do.

Give me a pill.

Can't afford the great reward.
Nothing to save, nothing to horde.
Make me a noose from that electrical cord.

Or give me a pill!

THE HEAT IS RISING

The heat is rising. Stir the pot,
Let it boil to the top.

The earth is turning.
Trees are burning.

Climate change?

Ice will melt in the sun.
People's reaction will be to run.

The sky's a-falling; spread the news!
Send money to pay the dues.
Follow man and sing the blues.

Before the end, you'll have to choose.

Before the end, you'll have to choose.

Before the end, *you have to choose!*

POLITICS AND FAITH

I am sure that you can tell from my writings that I am frustrated with church. I have frustrated a pastor or two as well. I continue to work out my salvation with fear and trembling. I am a work in progress.

I feel a desperation for people, and I am somewhat fearful that over the next two election seasons, people will get comfortable with the goodness God is about to bestow upon this nation. I pray that instead of relaxing, the church will get desperate, people will be thankful, and they will recognize that God is the giver of the bounty. He controls the atmosphere. This is not a time for rejoicing but for lamenting. In desperation people cry out, "Abba, Father," but in times of plenty they forget.

I was sitting in Bible study on a Wednesday night in 2013 and God began to give me a vision: a large tree growing up through the White House. The tree had pale bark and many leaves, with roots growing deep. This tree was to bring relief to the people, and the nation would thrive. This tree would serve one term. There was to be a second tree growing up through the White House from the same shoot, but this tree would be taller with more leaves, deeper roots, and abundant fruit. I believe this tree will serve two terms. This will not be a time for rejoicing but for testing, for pruning, and for purging.

Where there are rumors of revival, be leery, for if humankind is the star of the show, there will be no Holy Spirit. You will be entertained by imposters. Watch and listen for fires of revival breaking out across the earth. The true revival will bring people to their knees in repentance and worship. When God moves in close, every knee will bow and every heart will be dismayed as His presence illuminates sin. This is not to make a person feel bad or ashamed but the opposite. God illuminates the darkness so that we can be free to live in the light. He desires for us to draw so close to Him that communication is done without words, spirit to Spirit, heart to heart. His love for us is fierce. As His bride we must be purified, so I say, let the burning begin ... *in me!*

As a Christian, I believe it's my responsibility to pay attention to the political control of my nation, state, and community. The government threatens the tax-exempt status of a church if the particular church is political. Separation of church and state was meant to keep the laws separate from the religion. Sharia law is a great example of religion interfering with state or national law. No one should be exempt from the law of the land. You may follow your faith and live out your beliefs as long as you don't break the law, committing murder, engaging in theft, abusing your spouse or child(ren), speeding, drunk driving, etc. These are laws put in place to protect all citizens.

Discussing one's civic responsibilities and the state of the nation should be a natural thing in the church. Decisions made by our politicians affect our lives and the lives of future generations. Until Jesus comes back, our freedom to worship God is in jeopardy. There are liberal and conservative Christians alike, though I am not sure how. Every Christian should know the Word well enough to determine or to discern what God is saying about the state of our nation. The Bible has declared the victory and revealed the decline, so we shouldn't be surprised by what is happening. The world is full of unsaved people. Our job as Christians is to deliver the message, cast out the demons, heal the sick, and care for the widows and orphans. There are those who believe that our faith and trust should be placed in the government. Of course these are the people who work for the government and who excuse themselves from things like Obamacare. Some believe they are called to serve us, but they are doing their best to force all people into one belief and forcing everyone to tithe into one basket for the government to distribute.

Christians are not called to be depressed or worried about the future. We are called to pray and fast for the lost and for our leaders. We are to pray for them to come to the full knowledge of Jesus Christ, and to have wisdom, revelation, and discernment. We pray for safety and peace over their lives despite their politics.

This one nation under God, misinterpreting the Constitution of the United States of America, uses our tax dollars to abort children, to educate murderers, to care for illegal aliens, and to support terrorists, all while ignoring the needs of our very own heroes. The riots over President Trump taking office are insane, and the insanity is encouraged by our elected officials!

At this time, 2017, hurricanes are raging one after another, fires are breaking out in California again, and an earthquake in Mexico has claimed over three hundred lives so far. Is God speaking? Does He seem happy? Regardless of what you believe, God is still in charge of the wind and the waves. Look around you and ask yourself what in the world He would have to happy about.

SNAKES AND DRAGONS

Snakes and dragons hide in a hole.

Truth is buried deep in the soul.

"I don't know."
"I don't recall."

Hold up a wall washed in deceit.
Each lie, another repeat.

"I don't know."
"I don't recall."

In time the guile will rise to view,
Exposed to those you are subject to.

"I don't know,"
"I don't recall,"
Will be your downfall.

It's me you serve.
My money you spend and splurge.
I'm calling for a purge.

I do know and I do recall;
Each lie that you deny is writing on the wall.

Beware of the hand that you can't see.
Beware of the person you're trying to be.
Beware of the snake that hides in your tree.

For in the end, all will be revealed.

WOMEN

It's extreme to want to end abortion—
A war on women—

But natural to butcher the unborn.
Choice for the living.

Life is in the blood.

From sea to shining sea,
Our shores begin to flood

With dead bodies.

Save the seals, save the whales,
Save the lions, and save the snails!

But kill the babies.

Crucifixion without the nails.

We will all give account of the bodies we've buried.
We will all give account of the demons we've married.
We will all feel the weight of the burdens we've carried.

Innocent Blood

Pray for the blood that runs through the city
From under the butcher's door.

This little girl who used to be pretty
Isn't pretty anymore.

Out in the street she looks to repeat
As the numbers begin to soar.

Parts for pay, and by the way,
There's a smell of death and decay.

The spirit of murder lives deep in the soul.
There's nowhere to bury the bones.

The love of God can make you whole
And halt the deadly stones.

It's never too late, not with Him.
He loves you too, you know.

The world will say to hang on tight,
But God says, *"Let it go!"*

Fact From Fiction

I serve an amazing God, and I want to share Him with everyone I meet. In this day and age, it is hard to tell the truth from a lie, fact from fiction. It is getting harder to determine what is good and what should be considered evil. Racism is at an all-time high, and demonstrations are far from peaceful. Terrorists are set free, aiding in the growth of global terrorism. At times it feels as if our leaders are being more loyal to other nations than to their own. A pastor shouldn't be more concerned with how he looks to the community than how he looks to his own sheep. Our kids go to university for an expensive education and come out indoctrinated with socialist values and the idea that free speech is only free if it glorifies socialism. We pamper killers, detained jihadists, allowing them to have prayer essentials, to grow beards, and to have special foods and time for their rituals, yet we crucify students, coaches, or graduates who pray and give God honor or who speak the name of Jesus.

I cannot make you believe in God or in Jesus. I cannot give you my faith or my joy, and I cannot prove God to you. If you do not see or hear God in me, then I am probably not who I should be either. What I can do is encourage you to seek Him until you connect with Him. Ask God to reveal Himself to you and He will. Don't just ask once and give up; let Him know that you are serious.

The state of our nation is everyone's business and has everything to do with our faith. If your church has to give up its tax-exempt status in order to operate in the political realm, know that it's only money. God provides, and He makes all things work together for our good.

ALLEGIANCE

I pledge allegiance to the USA,
To the soldiers who fought and paved the way
For the freedoms we enjoy today.

Thank you, men, and women too,
For all you've done, for all you do.

You sign on the line, put my life first.
Some of you die, and some of you get hurt.

It's you who make me feel secure
At a time when I'm not really sure.

This nation, far from pure,
Is losing ground and the hope for a cure.

Integrity is but a blur.

So draw a line in the sand,
Like Jesus did with His hand.

Under God take your stand.
Declare this nation to be holy land.

EDUCATION

Movers and shakers and complacent takers.

Lovers and liars, professional fakers.

Man-haters, eliminators, first-raters.

Spiritual eradicators.

Dominators.

Mighty educators.

THE TRUE MEANING OF CHRISTMAS

Atheism has experienced a growth spurt. There are billboards encouraging Christians to skip church on Christmas Day, saying that the celebration of Christmas is about giving gifts and spending time with family, and claiming that it is a holiday for everyone that has nothing to do with Christianity or the Savior, Jesus.

If you are not a Christian, why are you celebrating? Why not just take your days off, save money, time, and stress by eliminating gift giving, and go on vacation? No one forces you to celebrate, yet you demand that the true meaning of Christmas be silenced or eliminated. Christmas is a Christian holiday celebrated by Christians. It is a joyful time of year, a time of hope and peace, yet it is an irritant to those who do not believe. So if you don't believe, don't celebrate, don't sing, don't go to church, and don't be merry. I will pray peace and good tidings for you and for yours, but I will not allow you to rob me of my joy.

Atheists have the right to put up their billboards and to demonstrate against Christmas. What aggrieves me more are Christians who treat Halloween like a holiday and Christmas like an event. And then the focus of Easter is on one's outfit, egg hunts, and stuffed bunnies.

We have woven so much pagan tradition into the fabric of our faith that it's no wonder atheists and other nonbelievers do not take us seriously. Thanksgiving has practically been eliminated, and at the very least overshadowed by Black Friday deals, getting the tree up, stringing the lights, and blowing up the giant Santa for the front yard.

Up and down the streets of my neighborhood, there are nativity scenes in many yards at Christmastime. It is a wonderful thing to see.

It's Christmas

It's Christmas. Let me be.
Stop trying to tweak the faith in me.

Hallelujah to this holy of nights.
We put up a tree and fill it with lights.

Some may say it's pagan.
To others it's a day off with pay.

Some are offended by the mention of Christ
But celebrate Christmas anyway.

I like to say "Merry Christmas,"
Which I also like to hear.
You can't deny that most reply
With a grin from ear to ear.

Why hate and debate?
Why cause a scene or humiliate
Those who permeate blessings?

He loves you too, you know,
No matter the seeds you sow.

Christmas is a daily choice
To walk in love or to use your voice,
To bless and praise in truth and grace,
To give the Spirit His holy place.

Belief in Jesus is not in my head.

I had the world but chose Him instead.

CHRISTMAS CONFUSION

I'm up,
I'm down,
All over the map.
For whom to buy this; why to buy that?

I've spent miles on line, used credit for gas,
Blown every single shopping pass.
All I want is a nap.

My tree's very tall and full of delight.
The presents are wrapped;
The bows are tied tight.

Oh God, I need a flight
To anywhere out of sight.

I'm not very lovely or loving these days,
No time for Christmas, no room for delays.

Parties and dinners,
Making up tales.
I need a new outfit.
Lord, let there be sales.

Gift exchange,
Trade a name.
Set the limit;
Play the game.

It's all so lame.
Santa Claus gets all the fame.

We're overstuffed and overbuffed,
Overpuffed and overfluffed!
Where is Jesus in all this stuff?!

We put on pageants to re-create
The scene of His birth,
To celebrate.
The date—

That's even up for debate!

So this year in honor of Him,
Right a wrong and make a new friend.

Give to the poor and help the needy.
Pray for the lost, the helpless, and the greedy.

Love one another, but love God first.

Rejoice and sing. Let the bells ring.
A Savior was born to become our King!
Death has lost its sting.

What other reason is there to sing?

CHRISTMAS

Red and green, a glowing scene.
What's it all mean?

A tree, some lights, a package tied tight.
Decorate,
Celebrate,
Accumulate, only to deflate.

I reason the season has meaning beyond
A merry greeting or singing a song
About snowmen and Santa,
And reindeer that fly.
Sugar plums, romance, eggnog, and pie.

"A holiday?' you say. "Let's have a parade."
Honor the jolly guy in the sleigh.
Children believe he'll bring presents their way.

The only gift important to me
Is the gift of life that's given for free.

Jesus—He's the one who died for me.

THANKSGIVING

Thanksgiving feast, stuff the beast.
Thanks for the peas and the carrots.

We sit to dine then pour the wine,
Discuss our trip to Paris.

As the plates are filled, we're dying to eat.
The prayer starts with Uncle Pete.

"Thank you, Lord, for my new Ford.
Thank you for good health.
Thank you, God, for my new job.
Thank you for the wealth.

"Thank you for a wonderful family,
Such a blessed life,
Even though all morning
I've been fighting with my wife."

Around the table, all who are able
Give thanks.

It's good to be thankful, but let's not forget,

It's not the things or even good health,
Not about family or having wealth.

For no person is richer than one who knows

The One who died for all our souls.

Halloween

All Hallows' Eve.
What do you believe?

It's no big deal and not for real.
O the webs we weave.

Religion is naive.

The pitter-patter of children's feet,
Begging for candy from people they meet.

Witches and demons,
Fairies galore.
Heroes and villains;
We buy out the store.

As children lie at night in their beds,
Flying monkeys dance in their heads.

We romance the demons,
Ouija the board,
Seek the Magic 8-Ball to aggrieve the Lord.

Don't ya think that

It's time to cut the cord?!

The Faithful

Would you remain faithful to God if you were imprisoned because of your belief in Jesus? Could you rejoice for being beaten and spit on because of your faith in Christ Jesus? Watchman Nee, who died in 1972, spent most of his life in a Chinese prison. It stuns me that this kind of thing still happens. Watchman Nee spent his time in prison writing and teaching people about the importance and power of the Holy Spirit. He already knew his Bible from intense study when he was free, so writing from prison without a Bible was a natural thing for him. He did not complain; he endured, and he worshipped the Lord.

People go on mission trips and find that people from other countries love Jesus better and know Him better than we Americans do. Many a missionary has been shocked to find that their faith was shallow in comparison to that of Christians in other areas across the map. People from other countries actually risk their lives to love Jesus. Depending on where you are, people lose their jobs, their homes, and their lives because of Jesus. They are the real deal. We are so spoiled in this country that we worship every goofy thing but God.

We devalue life everlasting, the Crucifixion, and the blood. We water down salvation and repentance, and ignore the Holy Spirit. We wonder why church is dry and lifeless. We have even turned a testimony into a "story."

So who is the church? I can tell you that after a year of studying the Word and going through deliverance, I was led by God right to the church. I'm not talking about the building full of people; I am referring to the church, the small community of people who recognize God's voice and obey Him.

> Jesus answered, "I am the way and the truth and the life.
> No one comes to the Father except through me. If you

really know me, you will know my Father as well. From now on, you do know him and have seen him." (John 14:6)

Very truly I tell you, whoever believes in me will do the works I have been doing, and they will do even greater things than these, because I am going to the Father. (John 14:12)

If you love me, keep my commands. And I will ask the Father, and he will give you another advocate to be with you forever—the Spirit of truth. (John 14:15)

Jesus is the Word in human form. How can you mimic someone's life if you don't know how they lived, worked, talked, or responded? The Word of God is our atlas, our training manual, our study guide, a living testimony of our Savior. No matter how many times I read the Word, I learn new things. I ask the Holy Spirit to fill me and to guide me through the Word. I ask Him to reveal what's hidden. I knock when I stumble across something I'm having trouble with, and God opens the door to reveal the truth. I seek all that God has for me, and that's what He wants from us. He loves to surprise me with new revelation or enlightenment so as to keep me coming back for more.

This is a relationship, not a onetime deal. I don't know what your religion is or where your faith level is, but I do know that the Word tells me to work out my salvation with fear and trembling, because it is God who works in me to will and to act according to His will. My textbook is my Bible, and the teacher is the Holy Spirit—God.

We come to Jesus just as we are. We may be born again, but the sanctification, the regeneration, the refining, and the training has just begun.

Philippians 2:12 tells us to do everything without complaining or arguing. However, it means much more than that. If you start from the beginning of Philippians 2, you see that there is much instruction for us and there is always an action expected of us. It is easy to say that God is love and to leave it at that, but you need to ask yourself how much you love Him. At the beginning of chapter 2, Paul says that *if* you have any encouragement from being united with Christ, *if* you have any comfort from his love, *if* you have any fellowship with the Spirit, *if* you have any tenderness and compassion, then make His joy complete by being like-minded, having the same love as He has, being one with Him in spirit and purpose.

If is the keyword here. Just because you asked Jesus to be your Savior doesn't mean you have a relationship with Him or are obeying Him in any way. God has a purpose for every one of us who repents and surrenders our lives to Christ; however, even after the moment of salvation, we make choices that will either draw us close to Him or drive us away from Him. A born-again Christian filled with the Holy Spirit of God, anointed by the Spirit of God, can still choose to open a door for Satan. The enemy is always looking to devour those who belong to God. The unsaved are already his to toy with; they are already deceived. The enemy won't cast himself out or fight against himself; there is no war there. He is looking for Christians to confuse, to tempt, to corrupt, to hold back, to take back, to destroy.

So are you a Christian? How do you know? Is Jesus the Lord of your life? Does taking Communion make you saved? How about your church attendance, being chosen for leadership, tithing, giving to missions? Exercising your flesh is not spiritual unless you are being led by the Spirit of God. A born-again believer will talk differently, respond differently, even dress differently, and will know that this life is no longer about them.

Jesus died on the cross for you. You cannot save yourself. If we are all little gods, then why did Jesus have to stand in for us? If we are so capable, then why are we to depend on and obey the Holy Spirit? If we are good just the way we are, then why are we to put off the flesh and become a spiritual people, a new creation?

> Jesus replied, "Anyone who loves me will obey my teaching. My Father will love them, and we will come to them and make our home with them. Anyone who does not love me will not obey my teaching. These words you

hear are not my own; they belong to the Father who sent me." (John 14:23)

If you think a demon or demons can't inhabit the house of a Christian, then you are deceived. Look around your sanctuary on Sunday and tell me that it is free of adultery, idolatry, lying, cheating, addiction, pride, and arrogance, even murder.

WALKING ON WATER

W ould you rather be trudging through the mud or sinking in quicksand, or does walking on water sound better? Walking on water sounds like fun. The other two options seem like a lot of work—very stressful and potentially dangerous.

Jesus walked on the water. So did Peter. Jesus told the disciples that the things He did, they would also do—and that they would do even greater things. I am thinking He meant greater things at greater levels for God to receive greater glory!

When Jesus healed, He didn't ask if the person was saved. He *knew* their level of faith without asking. They had heard of Him or had witnessed the things He had done for people. When they came to Him, they didn't have a laundry list of problems and needs, and they didn't talk His ear off explaining every detail of every issue. One woman simply pushed through the crowd and touched the hem of His robe. Her faith was so powerful and her desperation so raw that He felt it! Where did Jesus feel her faith? In His heart! She touched Jesus's heart. She didn't fill His head with negative, selfish, pitiful words. She simply touched His heart with her faith.

The hem of the robe was where all the mud and the camel and donkey poo was. The woman was desperate. She fought through the crowd, so she may have been growling a little even, or grunting to get through the people, but she made it. She made it to the hemline, at which most people would have turned their noses up and instead waited for an opportunity to touch His arm or His hand. Some would argue that she touched the hem of his shawl around his shoulders. That may be the case. However, when I read this part of scripture, I feel desperation and I see the woman low to the ground. If the crowd was large and tight, the only way to go would be low.

People tell me often that everyone has their own interpretation of the Bible and that this is why there are so many different denominations.

Walking on the water does not mean that all your prayers answered the way you want them to be answered, or getting everything you ever wanted. Walking on the water is about living *in* Christ. It is about being able, in any circumstance, to find rest and peace *in* Christ. Walking on the water is trusting God in every circumstance and in obedience. Desiring His will above everything you have ever thought, planned, schemed, and dreamed means living *in* peace, love, faith, grace, mercy, and truth.

Walking on water is about overcoming fear. Life can throw you a curveball or two, but when you are walking on the water, you know that He knows and you trust the one you belong to. God doesn't want to give us the desires of our hearts. When we are born again, our desires are selfish and flesh driven. When we surrender all, we are allowing God to give us new desires, desires that match His. I desire to know God and to obey Him. I desire to come to a full knowledge of Jesus Christ—the Word. I desire to fellowship daily with the Holy Spirit of God in order to touch God's heart and see the way He sees. I certainly did not have those desires before I got saved.

Do I daydream about having a new pair of shoes on occasion? Yes I do. I am still a human on the earth, living in the flesh, so yes, I love shoes. Nevertheless, none of us should allow things to come between us and God. If you want to fulfill the great commission, then you have to sign up for boot camp. The Holy Bible is your training manual. The entire Bible is about growing, changing, striving, running and walking, obtaining and defending, fighting and loving, giving and taking, losing or winning, and standing or resting. There are action words wherever there is a promise. Our action or inaction determines much and reveals much about who we are and what our position is in Christ.

For those who love Him, for those who believe, for those who obey, fight, stand, speak, hold their tongue, guard their heart, take every thought captive, sharpen their sword, pray, fast, seek His face, honor Him, praise Him, worship Him, glorify Him, are thankful ... He will. He will do it, going above and beyond anything we can imagine. His blessings are for our benefit and are always on time.

Just because I can't yet step out onto the lake and keep from sinking doesn't mean that I won't someday.

A True Encounter

❖⸺⸺⸺⸺◆⸺⸺⸺⸺❖

Meanwhile, Saul was still breathing out murderous threats against the Lord's disciples. He went to the high priest and asked him for letters to the synagogues in Damascus, so that if he found any there who belonged to the Way, whether men or women, he might take them as prisoners to Jerusalem. (Acts 9:1–2)

We all know Saul's testimony; he got saved on the way to Damascus. Saul had the type of encounter with God that I pray everyone will have. Saul was present during Stephen's stoning and approved of the action. Saul had a heart for his religion and for a God he didn't really know. He also had the heart of a killer. He thought he was protecting God by hunting all who believed in Jesus. He intended to return to Jerusalem with Christians, and his plan for them once he got there was not a good one. Saul referred to those who believed in Jesus as "the Way." I have come across the Way many times in my search for spirit and truth in worship and fellowship. The Way believe and experience; they see and hear; they know God, and He knows them.

It is not about how well you preach or prophesy or pray. God's people listen to and obey the Holy Spirit, and He is able to do many wonderful and miraculous things among them and through them. It is He who adds to the number daily those who are being saved. God will not share the sanctuary with your dragons. He is there to clean house, not to pacify the sinner.

What else could fool the church so easily? Who discerns sin inside the walls of your sanctuary? Jerusalem was the center of religion. God used religion to kill Jesus. Christians are deceived by religion every day. The Bible is addressing Christians. Who else would be reading the Holy Bible? The world is already deceived, so whom does that leave? Christians will be led by their arrogance, laziness, and greed through a promised salvation by denomination.

When will you stop having doubts about God? When will you be able to share a testimony? When will you be able to hear the voice of the Lord? When will you come to the full knowledge of Christ? Not until you pick up the Word and read it for yourself! Jesus tells us that He is the *Way*, the truth, and the life. He is the Word who came to life.

The Israelites roamed around the desert for forty years, and no matter how many signs, miracles, and wonders they witnessed, or how much provision they received from God, they did not get it.

Jesus died to save us. You cannot save yourself, and no person can save you. If you could save yourself, Jesus wouldn't have had to die on the cross. If religion could save you, then why were the Jews in slavery, nearly annihilated a few times, persecuted, tortured, and crucified?

God's church seems to be blurring the lines, skewing the truth, and making excuses for ignoring basic principles and discretion. Instead of being truthful for God's sake, we skirt around the truth for people's sake. Whom is this helping?

Do you hear from God? Would you recognize His voice if He spoke to you?

Do we need a hook to reel people in to our church building, or do we allow the Holy Spirit to draw people to His presence? I know I sound like a broken record, but you should be hearing this very basic teaching from the pulpit of your church on Sunday morning. This is basic Christianity.

Jesus and the apostles went out, found a place suitable for a crowd to gather, and preached. Simple. They taught in spirit and in truth, and they worshipped in spirit and in truth. Can you imagine the worship back then? They certainly didn't have a sound system, and I'm sure they worked with crude instruments, and yet God added to their number daily those who were being saved. Many were delivered of their demons and healed of sickness and disease, their minds becoming sound, leading them to become part of the church.

When the Holy Spirit is given the lead or headship, change takes place. The Holy Ghost is God, in case you didn't know. I have come across many churchgoers and Christians who do not know that God is the Holy

Ghost. I would say that most people who attend church don't hear much about the Holy Spirit or of being baptized in the Holy Spirit and fire.

Why do you keep a distance between yourself and God? I think we all do to some degree because we are none of us perfect. The truth is that God calls us to repent, to surrender the dark, secret places within ourselves to Him, so that we can go from glory to glory. He wants to draw close to you, and He wants you to desire intimacy with Him.

> Intimacy: a close, familiar, usually affectionate or loving personal relationship with another person. A close association with or detailed knowledge or deep understanding of a place, subject, period of history, etc. An act or expression serving as a token of familiarity, affection, or the like. An amorously familiar act. Sexual intercourse. The quality of being comfortable, warm or familiar.

The Holy Spirit dwells in us starting at the point of salvation. His job is to relieve us of our sin, fears, worries, doubts, and addictions. The more we "release" or surrender to Him, the more testimonies we have to share with others for their sake. We are supposed to change, to become better, to reflect Jesus. Isn't that the goal? God will not dwell where sin abounds. Trust comes through the fire.

Where are you in relation to God? Are you satisfied? Do you think that only some are anointed? I tell you that all who desire God and His will, who seek to find answers, who knock to discover, and who ask in faith will come to a place of knowing and will come under His anointing. You don't need a pulpit, a microphone, or a guitar; God will use you mightily in your home, on the job, in your prayer group or Bible study, at your children's preschool, or in the PTA! He is looking for conduits or willing vessels to operate through.

How do you obey God? I would say the best place to start would be to read the Word. If you are born again, you will begin to understand what you are reading. I ask the Holy Spirit to open my understanding and to teach me.

I think it is exhilarating to know that our mission on this earth covers a much larger piece of ground than just our little corner of the world. Fame and fortune are not bad things, but they do come at a price. Jesus is the famous one in a Christian's world. He provides a door for us to enter, and beyond that door is the spiritual power, wisdom, knowledge, and discernment. It is He who saves, but He uses our arms, legs, mouth, ears, heart, and hands to build His kingdom on this earth. Not your kingdom, church, or ministry: His.

Everybody wants to go to heaven, but nobody wants to die. As I write these pages, I am reminded of all the ways I fall short daily. Thank You, Jesus, for revealing truth to me so that I may be set free!

Proverbs 8:17 reads, "I love those who love me, and those who seek me find me."

Proverbs is the book of wisdom. I recommend people read from Proverbs until they are wise enough to handle the book of Psalms. New Christians get caught up in the psalms and wallow in self-pity for way too long. Many of them never move forward because they would rather read about being rescued over and over than take responsibility for either their mistakes or their salvation and relationship with God. The truth is that we all have a past and we all have pain that we need to overcome. The psalms offer comfort and are confirmation of God's faithfulness, love, protection, and provision. We need both the book of Psalms and the book of Proverbs to bring spiritual balance.

Proverbs prepares us for battle and change. Proverbs helps to establish a righteous base, so that in both hardship and blessing we are equipped and prepared. It provides a focus and right response for every situation.

HOW DO YOU KNOW?

M any people call themselves Christians and attend church regularly. Many people follow the pattern of tithing, serving in a ministry, and even using the Ten Commandments as their life guide. Most people who call themselves Christians have at some point been baptized in water before their assembly. Many churchgoers attend seminars, attend conventions, go on mission trips, and even do charitable work in their communities.

How do you know that you have been born again? How has God changed you, and would anyone else, including your family, attest to the changes? What is your relationship with the Lord really like?

Many think that the day they were baptized in water was the day of salvation. It could happen, but did it? Some think that when the priest laid hands on them and anointed them with oil, they were anointed by the Holy Spirit. It could happen, but did it? Some believe that when they were sprinkled as an infant, they became born again. It could happen, but did it?

I have talked with many churchgoing people who never read their Bibles. My question to them is, how can you know Jesus if you never read the Word? Jesus is the Word. Many ask, "What about a person stranded on an island without a Bible?" The Lord appears to us in many ways, but if you are not stranded on an island, why wouldn't you want to know the one who saved you? I would think you would want to get to know His character and attributes. Don't you want to know what He says about you?

God increases our understanding if we are faithful to seek the truth. Seeking the truth never ends. I don't know how many times I have read the Old Testament or the New, but I can say that I learn something new and fresh every time I read the Bible.

Early in my salvation I would run across the street with my Bible and ask my friend Jane if she knew that the Bible said this or that. She would giggle and say, "Yes, I think I have read that. Would you like to talk about it?" Or she would simply tell me to keep reading, because she recognized that God was illuminating the Word to me. She would only step in if she was instructed to by the Holy Spirit to do so.

As a new Christian, I started in the book of John, per Jane's direction. I eventually made it back to Matthew, Mark, and Luke, which I have read many times over the last twenty years. You will not grow as a Christian if you do not read the Word. You may make some changes to your personality and habits, but you will not grow spiritually if you do not read the Word of God and receive from it. Spiritual maturity must happen if one is to achieve unity with the true church and within the church. It is your job as a Christian to come to the full knowledge of Christ. The church should be a force to be reckoned with, a place of safety and power, not where you go to get your diaper changed or to refresh your bottle.

We are not called to cooperate with the world, so why do we? We live in the world but we are not to be of the world. We are called to be a spiritual people because our life is found beyond this realm. Our life is Jesus, and our communication with Him is spiritual through praying, fasting, and reading the Word. This may be difficult to understand, but how were you expecting to communicate with God?

I have assumed far too much since my salvation. I used to live with the fantasy that church was a clean and pure place where only the best people were allowed. I have since discovered that church is a building full of people in need of deliverance and healing.

We are a nation of addicts, whether our drug of choice is methamphetamine or pain pills, Prozac or Thorazine, gambling, sex, pornography, eating, spending, golfing, running, drinking, smoking, spending money, controlling people, lying, stealing, seducing, manipulating, abusing, engaging in self-pity, working, sleeping, molesting, committing incest, or raping—and the list goes on.

People are quick to say "don't judge," but I tell you that judgment starts in the house of the Lord! Judging the world is pointless because the world is deceived. Loving the church is work and takes courage. Successful relationships are honest relationships, being honest even to the point of risking the relationship. Being in right relationship with God is more important than sparing the feelings of someone who could die tonight while far from God. God is attracted to the broken and contrite heart. Are you broken? Are you convicted? Are you in pain or in need? Ask and you shall receive; seek and you shall find; knock and the door will be opened.

Some believe that a large portion of people in church are grazing sheep with their heads down, dependent on others to get them where they need to go. They believe that this group of people rarely tithe, rarely serve, and want a quick fix for all their problems. The body of Christ, the entire church, has value and purpose, but we have to mow the grass to get the sheep to look up! We must get their heads up and feeding on the Word. The Holy Spirit in us is life to our dry bones.

Edification is correction, direction, and encouragement. Before we encourage people to help in children's ministry, shouldn't we at least hear their testimony? Let's make sure that someone is really saved before we baptize them. We throw the sheep into ministry or into service without taking their spiritual temperature, only to find out once it's too late that they were not fit. God sends the sheep in to get help. If we are too busy worrying about the community outreach to feed our own sheep, what does that say about us?

A pastor once told me to come alongside him in leadership and to quit worrying about the lazy sheep. He told me to stop telling them everything. It wasn't long before that pastor began having meetings about me and my unwillingness to cooperate. He thought that if I would just read a certain book, it would change my mind and I would leave the sheep behind.

WHO IS THE CHURCH?

What does a Christian look like?

Where do I go to find the answers to the questions?

I think it is perfectly legitimate to ask these questions, because there are so many fellowships, so many doctrines, and so many beliefs that it can be confusing, especially for a new Christian.

Acts 3:19 reads, "Repent, then, and turn to God, so that your sins may be wiped out, that times of refreshing may come from the Lord."

I had been attending church for years and was not born again. I am sure you have heard the names: Bible-thumper, do-gooder, hypocrite. How about nosy busybodies with their own agenda; fake, two-faced drunks; lying gossips; and critical know-it-alls? I have used these terms myself, so why would I now want to be a part of that crowd? Does that sound like good fellowship?

The church is made up of flawed people with real life issues. Some are saved and some are not. Some are more spiritually mature than others, and some never take time to read the Word. None are perfect.

The job of Christians is to obey the leading of the Holy Spirit and to allow Him to bring forth His will through us. We are all called to pray and to give all our praise, honor, and glory to God. We are expected to support the fellowship with a cheerful attitude and generous spirit, and we are to be a light to those who are still in darkness. We are called to watch out for the enemy, to keep house, and to edify one another.

> Edification: building up of the soul, construction, a process, being uplifted, improved, correction or direction for moral improvement or guidance, to increase one's knowledge or to improve their character.

Being born again is the starting line, and the race isn't over until we reach heaven.

> For the word of God is alive and active. Sharper than any double-edged sword, it penetrates even to dividing soul and spirit, joints and marrow; it judges the thoughts and attitudes of the heart. Nothing in all creation is hidden from God's sight. Everything is uncovered and laid bare before the eyes of him to whom we must give account. (Hebrews 4:12)

> Living: means of support, subsistence, to keep, maintenance, sustenance, nourishment, daily bread, alive, live, having life, animate, sentient, active, thriving, vigorous, strong, flowing freely, burning, glowing, to feed, to dwell or reside in.

Aren't you tired of pretending that you're something or someone you are not? Aren't you tired of living with your glass half empty? The rich and the poor know that there is more to this life than money or wondering where your next meal is coming from. It is within all of us to know there is more, but how many of us actually know what the more is?

Why do some people seem closer to God than others do? What makes them so special? Nothing. I can tell you for sure that everyone who puts effort into any relationship will experience a more intimate connection with the other person. It is the same with God.

No one knows how to pray; we are all winging it. There is no right or wrong way to pray; however, we all need to ask the Holy Spirit to pray through us so that we hit our target. Just talk to Him, ask questions, anything—just open the lines of communication. What do you have to lose?

Read Ezekiel 47, the first chapter, and you will get a glimpse of how God wants us to live. If you don't understand it, read it yet again. Just put forth some effort to get to know God a little better.

WHAT CAN I DO FOR YOU?

Do you go to church on Sunday,
Or is Saturday your day?

Do you worship the Lord on Wednesday night?
Does going to Mass make you right?

Do you pray at 3:00 in the afternoon?
Do you need a hat or a mat?

Do you wonder if God lives on the moon?
Do you even think about that?

I met God while I was driving.
He spoke what I needed to hear:

"Dear daughter, what can I do for you?"
He knew I was living in fear.

I've gone to church on Sunday.
I've gone on Saturday too.
I've gone to church on Wednesday.
I've tried to get a clue.

So what do I need to do?

Get up in the morning and say,
"Hello, God. What can I do for You?"

Do You Feel God's Peace?

Do you leave church service feeling good about yourself? Do you feel God's peace? Are you jealous of the relationship others seem to have with God? Do you understand the Word when you read it? Are you being changed? Are you closer to God than you were five years ago? Do you know Him any better?

There are worker bees in every fellowship, but I believe it is the minority who are obedient to God and who are producing real fruit. Among this group is where you'll find the heroes. They don't boast about their gifts, and they don't have to pray the loudest and the longest. They give of their time and money and don't expect a pat on the back. These people have discernment, and they are not easily fooled.

Why do these people seem so close to God? What makes them so special? Nothing—not to God anyway. He sees us all the same and He desires a relationship with every one of us. What sets these folks apart is the Holy Spirit and their love for the Lord. They have made their election sure. They have the living and active Word in them, and they have surrendered their wills to God. They work out their salvation daily, and they commune with God constantly.

> Jesus replied, "Anyone who loves me will obey my teaching. My Father will love him, and we will come to them and make our home with them. Anyone who does not love me will not obey my teaching. These words you hear are not my own; they belong to the Father who sent me." (John 14:23)

> "If anyone is ashamed of me and my words in this adulterous and sinful generation, the Son of Man will be ashamed of them when he comes in his Father's glory with the holy angels." (Mark 8:38)

Don't Give Up

Have I mentioned that Jane and her husband, Terry, prayed for five years for me to be saved? Obedience and dedication drove me into the arms of my Savior. I am very happy they didn't give up on me. Have you given up on someone? Did God tell you to? Five years is a long time to see no results, but they knew it wasn't about them or their comfort or their own wills. They laid their lives down each week for the neighbor who swore and drank and who "faked" her way through life. They were His arrows, and I was His target. Again, I am very glad they didn't give up!

The Bible doesn't need to be rewritten. The human experience transformed by the Word needs to be shared with the world. It is called a testimony. A testimony is the power of God affecting a human life, to the point that the old life belongs to someone you used to know. A testimony is victory over sin.

I understand when people say that church is full of hypocrites. I believe that is true. You don't have to be one of them. My relationship with the Lord is between Him and me. I believe that you need to respect and honor leadership. I have sat under leaders whom I loved dearly but with whom I could not be in spiritual unity. When I became frustrated and discouraged, God moved me on.

When leadership is a mixture of spiritual and nonspiritual men and women, there will be confusion and dysfunction. What is in the head is felt in the body. You may have five thousand members in your fellowship, but how solid is the foundation? How strong is the core? Is Jesus the hero? Is God adored?

My life before Christ and before marriage was very dark. My family did not go to church; we went the opposite direction. Witchcraft was practiced in my house off and on for many years. We sought psychics and practiced divination and sorcery, so I was familiar with the spiritual life.

I began to have visions and was hearing things in my spirit, so I went to Terry and Jane, my neighbors, who were growing Christians, and they took me to their pastor. I had been attending their church for about a year. I shared with the pastor that I had been waking up around 3:00 a.m. hearing a door slam and I would make my husband get up and check the house. The pastor then handed me a tiny book on intercession written by Kenneth Hagan. That little book set a fire in me. I realized that I wasn't crazy and that God was trying to get my attention. Now when I wake up to the sound of a door slamming, I get up to pray and intercede. It has been some of the most rewarding, most educational, most fun, and most intimate time I've spent with the Lord.

Every born-again Christian is called to the ministry of prayer. I don't care how you pray. Whether you pray in tongues or not, whether you pray out loud in front of others, you are called to *pray*! It is just a conversation with God. Communication is the key to every successful relationship.

Some nights my time with God is spent reading scripture and praying, and other nights there is warfare. I don't always know whom I am praying for or why. I just allow God to use me to intercede. I listen a lot more than I speak, and I try to obey quickly. God does not speak to me in long sentences; instead He uses very few words and makes use of mental pictures.

When we realize that God knows everything, we can relax and ask, "Okay, God, what do You have for me today?" When we trust Him with our lives, He can use us to help bring forth His will. It certainly doesn't hurt to express your fear and anxiety and admit your sin to God. Just don't forget to tell Him how much you love and adore Him as well. Most of our time in prayer should be praising Him and listening for Him to speak. He really does know our needs and our desires without our reminding Him of them every day.

Our minds will try to counteract the Holy Spirit because the mind is of the soul and is controlled by the desires of the body. I bind up confusion in the name of Jesus and I pray for a sound mind, the mind of Christ. I want to think spiritually and live like this life is just practice for the next. I ask God to fill me with His Holy Spirit and fire so that I may be in unity with Him and burn with His desire for the church and for the lost. I wait, and sometimes for a good while, but I tell Him that I am not moving until He moves me, and then only after confirmation.

There have been times when the confirmations come quickly, one after another, and times when they come over a period of time. I held a vision for over three years before God told me to release it. It wound up being four years by the time I obeyed.

I have had prayer partners and close friends whom I have shared visions and words with, and they have prayed with me. I have shared with them at times because I wanted to be checked. It takes a lot to deliver a message for the Lord concerning the church, especially if it is a rebuke, a correction, or a message giving direction. I have been called out for sharing, and so I have prayed. I am seeking the Lord's deliverance from any spirit that would entice me to gossip, to slander anyone, or to cause division. Such things are never my intention. Being a new Christian, I did not trust myself, so I asked for help.

No One Is Perfect

I knew a man who could quote nearly every scripture word for word and tell you where to find it in the Bible. I was immediately impressed, until I told him he could lead Bible study one week. It didn't take me long to realize that he had memorized scripture in his head but not in his heart. His accomplishment was more prideful than spiritual. He was being led not by the Holy Spirit but by the flesh. He couldn't lead because he had no real insight into the scripture; he had simply memorized the words. Every time someone asked him a question, he would snap back by quoting scripture, as opposed to relating to the person with the Word as well as with compassion.

There are so many different denominations and some of them are unbalanced. They produce radical behavior that is unlawful and certainly not scripture inspired. When leaders are found to be in blatant sin, when leaders refuse to deal with sin in the church, when humankind is the center of attention, and when money becomes the focus, the world sees. The world sees the church as a place of judgment but then will joke about seeing Christians bellying up to the bar or telling dirty jokes at work. The world watches as the adulterer leads the National Day of Prayer and the worship leader bails his kid out of jail again, asking for leniency. The world is sickened when the Christian begs for money to go on a mission trip yet owes everyone in town.

No one is perfect, and God's church is not perfect. We all fall short. However, shouldn't those who claim to know the Lord also reflect the Lord? Some would say that Jesus ate with the sinners, and I would agree. Yet He never sinned. He did not separate Himself from the world; He drew the world to Him. He didn't live like the world does; He set the better example, and as a result people were changed.

The divorce rate among Christians is shameful. Drug and alcohol use and abuse, adultery, lying, theft, coveting, jealousy and gossip, sexual sin and perversion, idolatry, control, arrogance, pride, and cliques are common things among so-called Christians. My argument with many of today's churches is, why are we ignoring these things and acting like things are okay? Why are we so afraid of offending someone when the sheep are in danger?

When sin is given rein, the body crumbles, the spirit flees, and desolate is the sanctuary.

James 2:19 reads, "You believe that there is one God. Good! Even the demons believe that—and shudder."

If you believe that you are born with a little Jesus inside of you and the only thing you need to do is wake that little Jesus up, I would say, Wake up and get the truth inside of you for real! Jesus is the Savior who died for our sins and who was raised from the dead so that you could be saved. Why did Jesus have to die if we could save ourselves? For that matter, who would need God? If you can save yourself, I guess there's no need to repent of your sins, because you don't need to be born again.

Jesus is the Word. Do you believe the Word? Or is the Word simply a good book written by people, with Jesus being the character of the book, a good example for us to follow?

We are born inherently sinners in need of salvation. Once we are saved, the Holy Spirit reveals God to us and works in us to turn a depraved soul into a righteous one. We are born in the image of God; we are not gods! Unless you take on a humble attitude and the attitude of a servant, you are deceived. And any teaching in opposition to the Word of God is heresy.

I repeat yet again, prior to my salvation I had dabbled in witchcraft, sorcery, divination, and enlightenment. My morals barely had a meter, and I had turned to alcohol for comfort. I lied and my entire persona was fake. I stole a small item when I was young, and that haunted me my whole life. I never stole again. I am not sure why that action weighed so heavily on my spirit, but I am glad that it did. I believe the heavy conviction from the theft was protection from God.

You are free to believe whatever you want, but if you need more proof that God is who He says He is and that Jesus is who He says He is, *ask*! What do you have to lose? You have much to gain if you will just *seek* the truth.

Don't think that because you are saved all your battles are over. We work out our salvation with fear and trembling. The Holy Spirit is our banner.

First Peter 1:5 reads, "Who through faith are shielded by God's power until the coming of the salvation that is ready to be revealed in the last time."

It is through faith that we are shielded against the enemy, who wants to destroy our salvation. Do you know the level of your faith? Why would God need to protect us if there was no danger of losing the hope of salvation?

> Therefore, with minds that are alert and fully sober, set your hope on the grace to be brought to you when Jesus Christ is revealed at his coming. As obedient children do not conform to the evil desires you had when you lived in ignorance. But just as he who called you is holy, so be holy in all you do; for it is written, "Be holy because I am holy." (1 Peter 1:13)

> Therefore, rid your selves of all malice and all deceit, hypocrisy, envy, and slander of every kind. (1 Peter 2:1)

"To sanctify" means "to make holy, to consecrate, to separate from the world, and to be set apart from sin so that we may have intimate fellowship with God and serve Him gladly." The sanctification process includes correction, direction, discipline, obedience, relationship, and repentance. A willing participant will morph into an amazing weapon for God, a minister of His grace, mercy, and love. We go from glory to glory through obedience and humility.

First Peter 2:11 reads, "Dear friends, I urge you, as foreigners and exiles, to abstain from sinful desires, which wage war against your soul."

If the deal were already sealed, regardless of how you live as a Christian, why would God need to warn us?

> Live as free people, but do not use your freedom as a cover-up for evil; live as God's slaves. (1 Peter 2:16)

Therefore, since Christ suffered in his body, arm yourselves also with the same attitude, because he who has suffered in his body is done with sin. As a result, he does not live the rest of his earthly life for evil human desires, but rather for the will of God. For you have spent enough time in the past doing what pagans choose to do—living in debauchery, lust, drunkenness, orgies, carousing and detestable idolatry. (1 Peter 4:1–3)

I encourage you to read 2 Peter 1:3–5. God has given us godliness *through* knowledge of Him. *Through* your knowledge of Jesus Christ, you may participate in the divine nature and escape the corruption of the world caused by evil desires. Make every effort to add to your faith goodness; and to goodness, knowledge; and to knowledge, self-control; and to self-control, perseverance; and to perseverance, godliness; and to godliness, brotherly kindness; and to brotherly kindness, love.

Second Peter 1:10 tells us, "Therefore, my brothers and sisters, make every effort to confirm your calling and election. For if you do these things, you will never stumble." *If* you do these things. I believe many who preach overlook the ifs so as to make the Word more tolerable.

Many Christians believe that they can't be manipulated or influenced by the demonic. Some believe that a Christian can't be controlled or inhabited by a demon after having been born again. If this is the case, then why does the Bible tell us to always be on the lookout and to resist evil? We are warned time and again that the devil roams around the earth looking to kill, steal, and destroy. You have to own something before someone can steal it from you, right?

There are people being used to usher in "the universal community church," where all is well, everyone is good, and all roads will eventually lead to heaven. I believe that many denominations or fellowships are being led into the all-inclusive church with one standard: love. Could this lead to the One World Church? God used the Jews to kill Jesus, and He used Judas, a disciple who lived and walked with Jesus, to betray Him.

OBEDIENCE

O*bedience* is a word used often in the Bible. In order to obey someone, you must be familiar with that individual. Anyone can follow the leader. The question is, do you have any idea where the leader is taking you?

I have never believed in the concept of once saved, always saved. How do you know you are saved? If you were saved when you were young, do you still feel saved? Do you know the Lord better today, or are you wondering why you even go to church? Do you pray?

Many have turned away from sound teaching, looking for a hook to win the lost. In the midst of shining your hooks, the saved are becoming bored with the entertainment and the soft, inoffensive speech. The saved have a need and a hunger to grow. They are serious about their relationship with the Lord. When a pastor designs his service around one group of people, he is not feeding the whole family. I would even say that he is not trusting the Holy Bible or the Holy Spirit. It is a case of a man trying to manipulate human beings while leaning on his own understanding.

Last Resort or First Call?

Why do we go to God as our last resort, when He should have been our first call? We develop relationships with people because we connect with them in some way. We make time for the people we care about, and we make an effort to learn more about them. We share bits of ourselves, and over time we form bonds. We text, call, visit, email, use Facebook, write tweets, use FaceTime, and more to keep our connections up to date.

We were created to communicate. God is relational and we are made in His image. For many, a relationship with God is a one-way conversation consisting of a list of demands or expectations and an exhausting menu of all our disappointments and pain.

Is your communication with God barely a blip on the screen, and only that on Sunday morning during church?

Talk to Him. Talk to God about everything that's on your mind and in your heart. This is all He is waiting for, and He has time for it. The Holy Spirit was sent down from heaven to be near us. He is waiting for you to respond to Him.

I tell God good morning and I ask Him to fill me with His Holy Spirit. I let Him know how much I love and trust Him and that I desire His will for my life. I ask Him to use me in any way He can to further His kingdom. That is the whole point of being born again. This life of mine is supposed to be about God's will, not my will. God has proven Himself. I have had to prove to Him that I am willing to obey. It is a two-way relationship.

God's Word tells us that when He sees that He can trust us with a little, He will give us more, more ministering opportunities, more insight, more knowledge, wisdom, revelation, discernment, peace, joy, and love. I have never been a bored or burned-out Christian because God keeps me busy. The more we are open to being trained and taught by the Word and Holy Spirit, the more usable we become.

We will all give an account of what we say and do, but we will also give an account of the things we don't say and don't do.

FIND YOUR PURPOSE

A s I am finishing writing *Where Are the Heroes?*, I am convicted of all the ways I need to be changed, of all the areas of my life that still need to be surrendered to God. My experiences are mine as I see them, and I am sure that my opinions are not representative of everyone. I don't want to agree to disagree. I desire unity in the spirit with God's true church, not with an organization or club. I am thankful that I did not come to Jesus indoctrinated with religion. While I admire those who grew up in the church, I pity those who live in a "God box" and never dip their toes in the water. There is always more with God, and until I die physically, I am going after the more.

I want to walk in such peace and faith that I never waver. I want to know and to have the faith to stand no matter what. Joy in the Lord isn't something you obtain; it becomes who you are, and it is revealed through the way you talk and respond and in the way you treat others.

If you are a part of the body of Christ, you have a purpose. God will use any vessel who spends time with Him. I can fill *Where Are the Heroes?* with scripture, and you may read over it, but the reason I am writing this is to get you to open the Word yourself. You need to search the Word for yourself and develop a hunger for the things of God.

I believe God's Word is simple. His expectations of us are simple as well. The Bible is filled with action words, and action is required of us. It is easy to read all the ways God desires to bless and protect us, and it is similarly easy to ignore our responsibility in the relationship. We tape feel-good scripture to our mirrors and admire our faces as we repeat the blessings of God over our lives. How about taping scriptures to your mirror that remind you to live a righteous life, to bless God with your every day and your dollar, and most all to walk in faith and thanksgiving?

He Opened His Eyes

There will always be wars and rumors of wars, but the Prince of Peace came so that we might obtain His peace, an inner peace that transcends all understanding. In other words, you could be going through the worst thing in your life, and to the world you should be angry, hopeless, or overcome by grief, yet even though you may grieve, you know that this life is not the end of the story. Trusting God can be the hardest thing you do.

We are distracted and at times fearful about what we see and hear. The prophet Elisha and his servant Gehazi were surrounded by the enemy. Elisha, knowing that Gehazi was fearful of what he saw, had faith that there were more with them than with the enemy. Elisha prayed for God to open Gehazi's eyes. When Gehazi opened his eyes, he saw God's army surrounding the enemy. Elisha then prayed that God would blind the enemy, at which point they became confused. Elisha knew God, and God knew Him.

Many battles are won through worship and repentance. The banner-bearers of Elisha's army went out to the battle lines first to declare the victory. The worshippers followed, praising God and declaring God the victor. The armed soldiers were the last to approach the enemy.

David faced a giant with a mere slingshot. David knew who was going to defeat the giant; he was simply the vessel.

In the presence of God, the angels sing as we repent, that sweet aroma of burning flesh reaching heaven.

†

Oh God, set the fires of revival across the globe
For the stubborn and contrite heart,
For the insane liar,

For the woman who murdered her child,
For the man who lay with his own daughter,
For the lover of money and self,
For the sheep who are seeking and the shepherd who has gone astray,
For the fatherless and the homeless,
For the lonely widow and the atheist,
For the witch across the street and the drunk in the bar.
Come, Lord Jesus, come.
Rescue the ones who have been deceived, the ones who know You little.
Rescue those in prison; bring them out of the dark.
Loose the strong hold on our minds and reveal the truth.
Heal our hearts and teach us how to live along the banks of the river.

Every day.

I Am Healed

Jesus died for me, so that makes Him the superest of heroes. When women come to my house for Bible study, my husband jokingly says to me, "You *Word* 'em, honey," because he knows how desperate I am to lead people into the arms of Jesus. God has used my house for ministry to the youth, to women, and to college- and career-age people because I walked its foundation, I walked the plywood floors, and I anointed the skeleton, and then the doorposts and window frames—and because I asked Him to. I dedicated my house to Him.

I owned and operated a private-duty home-care agency for twenty-two years, and I dedicated that business to Him, as well as ten percent of the gross income.

I could fill *Where Are the Heroes?* full of testimonies of God's goodness.

Anything worth having is worth working for and fighting for. My intercession for the church is that you will strive to know the Lord.

Just one month ago I was diagnosed with Parkinson's disease. I cried all the way home from the doctor's office, which I think is a normal response. I was looking out the window, thanking God that I didn't have cancer or a tumor or anything else that would be life-threatening. I began to see a clear bright picture screen, and running across that screen was my life. It wasn't going from beginning to end but from the present backward. It was running fast, but I could see all the ways that God has saved, provided for, protected, healed, changed, and blessed me. The screen was running fast, but I could see each thing very clearly. I smiled.

I had a car accident in June 1996, which led to my salvation. I was saved June 28, 1997. I went through deliverance in late June 1998, setting me free from all shame, guilt, witchcraft, and fear of Mother.

I do not believe in coincidences. When you study your Bible, you will see how important numbers, memorials, covenants, obedience, and worship are to God. I was diagnosed with Parkinson's in late June 2017, and I fully expect either to be miraculously healed or that a cure will be found in June of 2018 or 2019.

I will leave you with one of my favorite poems:

MARRIAGE

True romance is like a dance;
It moves the inner man.
With love you have to take a chance
And pray that it's God's plan.

Marriage is a promise; it's not a guarantee.

Some days you'll wish for boxing gloves;
Some days you'll want to flee.

No matter what the day may be,
For peace you'll have to fight.
The fun is in the making up,
Till everything's all right.

Be quick to say I'm sorry
And slow to light the fuse.
Be ready when the bottom drops.
Pray and don't accuse.

Be grateful when the fridge is empty;
Be grateful when it's full.
Be grateful when the car wears out
Or the shine is getting dull.

Hold hands and talk.
Sometimes take a walk.
Don't hide the things you need to say.

Be quick to pray.

Check Up

It would do us all good to check ourselves and our own spirituality regularly. I have listed several closing thoughts and questions for you to reflect on as you continue in the Word and in your walk with Christ. We cannot fear change, because change is what keeps us from becoming stagnant. Feel free to use these statements to help with your own personal change and to provoke change in others.

1. How can you know Jesus if you've never read the Word?
2. How can you sing love songs to someone you don't love?
3. If you've been born again, sharing your testimony should be easy.
4. Your spirit is at war with your mind. Which one is winning?
5. Acknowledge Him before humankind and He will acknowledge you before the Father.
6. No one can make you gossip. You have legs. Walk away.
7. You're only as weak as your prayer life. You're only as strong as your prayer life.
8. Self-pity is false humility; arrogance is self-importance.
9. A friend tells you what you need to hear, not what you want to hear.
10. What good is fellowship if it doesn't include Jesus?
11. You can preach a two-hour sermon, but is anybody changed by it?
12. You should measure success by the number of salvations, not the number of people filling the seats.
13. To exaggerate is to lie.
14. A testimony is a victorious account of what Jesus did to change your life; a story is about *you* changing *yourself.* And the wrestling match continues.
15. A spiritual parent spurs you on to serve the Lord, to obey the Holy Spirit.

16. A controlling spirit commands you to follow him or her.
17. Keep the sheep grazing and they'll never know what hit them when problems arise. Feed the sheep and you'll have a mighty army.
18. Whatever is in the head will flow through the body. Count on it.
19. It's not anyone else's job to make you "look good" to Jesus. When the two of you meet face-to-face, no one else will be there.
20. A relationship is developed. Maintaining it takes effort.
21. The person who leans on his or her own understanding will eventually fall over.
22. We are sons and daughters of the King, not beggars. If God is sending you, He will take care of the bill.
23. The plans of humankind are many, and they mostly come to nothing.
24. Discernment is the key.
25. Don't blame the devil if you belong to the Lord.
26. Be thankful in every situation.
27. Ask God to reveal His purpose in everything before giving the enemy credit.
28. The devil didn't pick Job; God recommended Job.
29. Eat the Word; it's the bread of life.
30. If you are looking for a blessing, be one.
31. If you can't receive correction or direction, you probably shouldn't be giving any.
32. God's plan for your life is in the Word.
33. There is only one road to heaven, and it runs through Jesus.
34. To divide the soul and spirit, you need a sharp double-edged sword.
35. Salvation is the beginning, not the whole package.
36. If you worry more than you worship, rebuke the worry and begin to worship.
37. Worry is a sin. Repent.
38. To obey is to follow the leading of the Holy Spirit.
39. Your pastor is not your source, he is a conduit.
40. Walk in peace; fight in the spirit.

41. Are you a warrior or a peacekeeper? Are you a peacemaker or an agitator? Are you a peacekeeper or a peacemaker? Do you know the difference?
42. The spirit of self-pity is high-maintenance.
43. Are you a giver or a taker?
44. Do you draw people or repel people?
45. Silence the watchmen and you will be clueless. Ignore the prophets and your house will be desolate.
46. You don't train someone to be a Christian; you are simply assisting God. Don't forget your place.
47. You are who God says you are.
48. White witchcraft or black witchcraft—they are both witchcraft.
49. Necromancy, divination, and magic all open the door to evil.
50. He is truth; it stings. He is oil; it soothes. He carried you until I could walk. He found you shelter—the church. He paid the bill—redeemed you. Pay it forward, Good Samaritan.
51. Obedience is how we love God.
52. Wisdom has legs; so does folly. They both try to control your feet.
53. Faith in Jesus is the power that heals.
54. If you treat the Holy Spirit like your morning coffee and the Word like your bacon and eggs, all will be well.
55. We were not called to cooperate with the world, so why do we?

THE MIRACLE

◆━━━━━◆━━━━━◆

As I was bringing *Where Are the Heroes?* to a close, my mother was diagnosed with aggressive lung cancer that had metastasized to the bones. Mother died early in September 2017. I was in communication with my brothers and asked if I should go see her. They told me she was very angry and belligerent, so I did not. I truly had peace in my own spirit and in my mind. I knew Mom would have pain, so I continued to pray for her salvation and for God to have mercy on her.

Three weeks prior to Mom's passing, the Holy Spirit began speaking: "Go see your mother." For three days I heard the same thing over and over. I called my brothers and asked if I should come, saying that I believed God was telling me to. I told them that it didn't matter what her reaction would be, because I knew God was telling me to go. They said then that I should come, so I lay down to take a nap and decided that I would go the next day. I could not sleep. When God wants you to do something, He gets pushy.

I got to the house. Two of my brothers and my niece were there. They told me to go on in and just see what would happen, adding that they were there for me. I went in and stood by the bed and waited. Mom opened her eyes and looked right at me. She began to wail loudly like a wounded animal. I started crying, fearing that I had caused her pain. I looked back. My brothers and niece were crying and telling me that it was good.

I began to stroke Mother's hair and to kiss her forehead as she continued to wail. The sound coming out of Mom was from deep within. It was painful to hear; I could feel her grief. I felt nothing but compassion for her. God has surely done a work in me. I kept saying that it was all okay now, that it was all over and the past was the past. I told her I was sorry for the way things were between us. When she calmed down, she put her hands on both sides of my face and pulled me close to her. Mom said that she saw hate in my eyes, and I told her, "No, I don't hate anyone."

"Maybe it's only when you look at me?"

"No, Mom, I don't hate you. I love you." And she started crying again.

I got six visits with Mom before she died, and in those visits my brother read the Word to her, we prayed with her, and she surrendered her heart to the Lord. She told me that she thought I had turned out to be a good person and that she was proud of me. Mom told me that she loved me, adding that I should never forget that.

In six visits I got to hold Mom's hand, kiss her, and tell her that I loved her. I also got to hear her bless me. I am fifty-seven years old and had never been hugged by my mother. It was awesome!

We have until our final breath to come to the Lord. When I see Mother again, it will be as if the old had never happened. Mom went through some deliverance and it scared her, but there were several of us there praying for her and witnessing the miracle.

How dare we give up on each other as if we are the ones who decide who should be saved? Jesus died for every soul. Prayer is power over darkness and a weapon against evil in this world, and we are all called to pray.

Printed in the United States
By Bookmasters